HOW TO MANAGE
YOUR GLOBAL REPUTATION

How to Manage Your Global Reputation

A Guide to the Dynamics of International Public Relations

Michael Morley

NEW YORK UNIVERSITY PRESS
Washington Square, New York

First published in the U.S.A. in 1998 by
NEW YORK UNIVERSITY PRESS
Washington Square
New York, N.Y. 10003

This book is printed on paper suitable for recycling and
made from fully managed and sustained forest sources.

Library of Congress Cataloging-in-Publication Data
Morley, Michael.
How to manage your global reputation : a guide to the dynamics of
international public relations / Michael Morley.
p.   cm.
Includes index.
ISBN 0–8147–5616–6
1. Public relations—Corporations.   I. Title.
HD59.M64   1998
659.2'89—dc21   98–13360
                                                                          CIP

Printed in Great Britain

■ Contents

■ Preface and Acknowledgements

There is no better time to make a career in international public relations. The planning and implementation of concerted multi-national public relations programs are still in their infancy. Global programs are, in truth, still a dream.

Similar conditions prevailed in 1967 when I met Dan Edelman and we agreed to establish a joint venture in the UK. London became the first city outside the USA with an Edelman office.

Friends pursed their lips. Won't this be a bit risky? What about the competition?

I had the arrogance of youth. I also had a mission to improve what I felt was a generally low standard of practice in British PR at that time. My reply, which I am still convinced was true, was: "Look, I only have to be mediocre by my own standards for our company to be an outstanding success." So it turned out, although I like to think we were better than mediocre.

And so it can be for those who really make an effort to succeed on the worldwide stage.

I hope this book helps.

You will quickly ascertain that this is not an academic work. It is in small part a memoir, a measure of historical color to help understand how we arrived at today's situation, some anecdotes and mostly, I hope, helpful information and tips. It is less a work of scholarship than lessons from first-hand experience.

There are many to thank for their vital contributions to this book.

First, my wife Ingrid, who had the patience of a saint when, at distant intervals, I sequestered myself to do the writing. But, more important, she was at my side during all the ups and downs over these past 40 years when I was gaining the experience that is, I hope, distilled in the following pages.

Second, thanks to Norman Hart, editor-in-chief of this series, and Macmillan, the publisher, for their extreme patience as first one deadline and then another slipped by without a finished manuscript, something that would have infuriated me if the tables had been turned.

Thanks to Dan and Richard Edelman for providing the environment for me to practice my craft and from whom I have learned so much, not just about public relations but about hard work and the business aspects of PR. And to my many colleagues and friends with whom I have worked over the years.

Special thanks go to the clients who have taken that huge step and entrusted their reputations and budgets to me and my firm. There have been moments (quickly suppressed) when I felt I should rebate some part of their fees because I learned so much from them.

What I have learned about international public relations I owe to having worked closely with a galaxy of outstanding practitioners, among them Jacques Coup de Frejac (France), Ramon Alvarez (Spain), Peter Czerwonka (Germany), Patrizia Antonicelli and Tony Muzi Falconi (Italy), Kaarina Alanko (Finland), Val McKenzie and Robyn Sefiani (Australia), Austen Zecha and Jeanette Robertson-Lomax (now Shahabuddin and living in Malaysia), Barbara Frischknecht (Switzerland, who died a few years ago), T.H. Lee (Korea) and Serge Dumont (China). David Davis, Rosemary Brook, Andy Knott and Susi Luss deserve special mention for many years of campaigning together. In recent years my professional horizons have been expanded by working closely with Pam Talbot, President of Edelman USA and Leslie Dach, a Vice Chairman of our company.

And I have been encouraged in the venture by my daughter, Ann Wool, who assisted me for a few years before spreading her wings on international PR projects of her own.

Without the help of three people, you would not be holding this book in your hand. Cathy Johnson played an important role in helping me get started. Paulette Barrett stepped in and not only acted as a sounding board and tough copy editor but condensed many of the case studies and pushed me to meet deadlines. Eneida Lamberty has organized the text, typed large sections which were initially produced handwritten and brought order to the text and the charts.

I had to make some decisions which may be offensive to certain groups. In the interest of attaining some flow of prose, I use the male gender to cover the entire spectrum. Thus he means she as well.

In the matter of monetary units, I have decided to work in US dollars to achieve some standard – at the time of writing, the Euro has still not arrived. And in spelling conventions, I have chosen American English rather than British, based on the toss of a coin and the fact that an American spell check function is built into the hard drive of my laptop computer.

■ Foreword

Never has public relations been so important to as many organizations as it is today. At the corporate level, we see public relations in action communicating corporate messages to the worldwide financial markets, shaping corporate images, telling "our side of the story" in times of crisis, and playing a key role in developing new identities and positioning for companies formed in the wake of mergers, acquisitions, and takeovers. At the brand level, public relations provides marketing support in the form of ideas for international, national, and local sponsorships, for cause-related marketing, and for brand-building via both consumer-directed and trade-directed communications.

It is not only for corporations that public relations has become more salient. A panoply of non-profit organizations, tourist development agencies, military services, and labor unions are among those who have harnessed public relations in their behalf.

Yesterday's public relations focused extensively on press releases; today's also involves video news releases and establishing and maintaining websites. Yesterday's focused on brand promotions; today's also emphasizes development and defense of corporate reputation. At its best, public relations is a component of corporate strategy.

This volume offers a comprehensive treatment of the field by Michael Morley, a highly experienced senior executive who has been engaged in public relations worldwide on behalf of companies and organizations for almost four decades. Morley's extensive collection of case histories is drawn from a wide range of industries and applications. They encompass programs in print and broadcast – and even the Internet. His frames of reference include both brand and corporate, and extend from individual firms to economic development agencies, trade associations, agricultural commodities, and causes.

Morley emphasizes the global character of business – and the public relations that support it – as well as the need to translate "big picture" programs into local initiatives. From a process perspective, he takes readers from strategy reviews through audits and issue identification/tracking to program development all the way to evaluation. He describes internal public relations organization and structure as well as the roles of the public relations agency.

From strategy to implementation, from the boardroom to the firing line, Morley provides insights for both the experienced and the aspiring in public relations.

Stephen A. Greyser*
Richard P. Chapman Professor
Marketing/Communications
Harvard Business School

* Professor Greyser is a director of several companies, including Edelman Public Relations Worldwide and Opinion Research Corporation

ix

CHAPTER 1

The Global Village – It's Here

The global village predicted 30 years ago by communications scholar and philosopher[*] Marshall McLuhan is here. The primeval forces that drive entrepreneurs to establish global empires have combined with those that enable them to achieve their ambitions.

The driving forces are the quest for survival, power, peace, pride and profit.

■ Survival

Company leaders know they must grow in size if they are not to be swallowed up by a bigger corporation. Even huge corporations that operate nationally or regionally are prey for the larger global corporate predators. The only solution for survival is to become global themselves, as fast as they can, through acquisitions, mergers or other forms of strategic alliances.

■ Power

Leaders of industry are just as hungry for power as presidents, prime ministers, generals and bishops. In today's business world, only the global corporation delivers the ultimate in industrial and commercial power.

■ Peace

Peace is a real motivation for those who believe that it may be easier to achieve or maintain when twinned with power. Many business leaders also believe that an economy in which nations are interdependent is a significant force for peace and that global corporations have a pivotal role to play in bringing that about.

■ Pride

Pride is often an overlooked motivation for globalization. For some individuals, the status conferred by being leader of a global corporation is sometimes more important than the power or profit that position brings. National rather than personal pride is a clear driving force for many of the huge corporations that emerged in post-war Japan and more recently in Korea and other countries which needed to reach parity with – and then overtake – companies in the USA and Europe.

* *The Global Village*, by Marshall McLuhan and Bruce R. Powers, published by Oxford University Press

Profit

Profit needs little elaboration. It is the primary reason for the existence of business enterprises. To achieve maximum profits, the corporation must operate on a global scale.

Technology, privatization, the dismantling of protectionism, swifter, cheaper travel, standardization and education have been important factors in helping business leaders achieve their global ambitions.

Technology

Technology has had a dominant impact on globalization. Its manifestations are the subject of many books on mass production, mass customization, production processes, training and so on. For public relations purposes, we need to recognize how technology has revolutionized communications, not just within business organizations but, most dramatically, in the media.

Privatization

With the retreat from Marxist socialism, many nations in the 1990s engaged in a wave of privatization of state-run and state-owned industries, opening the way to global alliances for institutions that had previously been strictly local.

Dismantling protectionism

Protectionist barriers have been taken down at a fast and relentless pace, notwithstanding media reports about counter efforts to prevent this trend in many countries. Free trade and groupings such as the GATT and its successor WTO, the European Union, Association of South East Asian Nations and North American Free Trade Agreement have enabled many companies to expand their international operations and stimulated mergers of nascent global corporations.

Travel

Travel is now faster, cheaper and accessible to more people than ever, facilitating the all-important, face-to-face meetings that remain a cornerstone of business, even in the global village. And that transport does not only carry people, it carries documents, packages and goods as well.

Standardization

Standardization has smoothed the way for products made in one market to meet the safety, size and ingredient requirements in a large number of other markets. With minor modifications, many products can be sold worldwide.

Education

Education has improved business leaders' knowledge of the history, traditions and languages of markets well beyond their home bases.

■ Media impact

With the premise that the global village has arrived, the PR practitioner should examine closely how this will impact his work. The Internet, television, telephone and radio have converged to take us into the age of instant communications, worldwide.

In the length of time it took news to circulate within a village of 200 people 200 years ago, it is now possible for five billion people to become aware of an environmental disaster, war or the outcome of a major sporting event. The Internet alone can disseminate news of a faulty or dangerous product to a worldwide audience in minutes.

The existence and speed of the new media should not be the only subject of concern for the PR practitioner. Its ownership is of equal importance.

The past decade has seen the emergence of powerful international media holding companies – Rupert Murdoch's News Corp, Time Warner, Disney, GE through NBC, Kirch and Bertelsmann in Germany, and Berlusconi in Italy. They all wield immense power nationally, regionally and, increasingly, internationally.

Companies that own media outlets are seeking to go global and to exercise greater control over content – news and programming sources. Those with their roots in print media have branched out into satellite and cable television, and vice versa. And all of them are making sure that they play a key role in use of the internet as the newest medium of all.

The trend toward consolidation alarms many who fear a world in which the concentration of media places commercial and political power in the hands of too few people. Yet a counter trend can be observed. Small groups gain unprecedented power with the advent of 500-channel television, and the capacity to produce professional-looking newsletters, magazines and even books that can be printed in small quantities. There are now newsletters, books and television programs that can serve very small communities, whether they be regions, villages, dialect groups or people with a shared interest in a sport or hobby.

Here, too, the Internet is a new medium with little editorial control, that returns immense power to the individual who, for one reason or another, does not communicate through the traditional major media groups.

■ PR practitioners for a new age

In the face of such a panoply of communications tools and opportunities, what sort of PR practitioner will we be seeing? What are the characteristics of the highest-ranking public relations professionals in the coming millennium? How might you plan to develop your talents to take a leadership position in communications, and perhaps beyond?

As you will read elsewhere in this book, public relations began by drawing its talents from other crafts and professions, mainly journalism but also from advertising, law, sales and politics. To be sure, it attracted its fair share of buccaneers and charlatans, who gave PR a flair and glamour that attracted many more professionals. Now, there are legions of practitioners who studied PR in college and have followed a career in the business ever since. Many of them have spent and will continue to spend their working lives in one of the PR specialties described in chapter 7.

In the future, I believe that the PR profession will continue to attract recruits from other fields – and will be the richer for it. They will come from all the same walks of life as before but there will also be more entrants from a variety of scientific backgrounds who have discovered in themselves a skill in communicating about their specialist fields.

It really does not matter what you study at college. It is no disadvantage to take a public relations course or program, usually run by the schools of journalism at various universities. This provides practitioners with a fast start in being familiar with the techniques of communication and the needs and structure of the media. But you could as well major in computer science, law, English or another language (or languages), political science or international affairs, and start work immediately in a communications capacity or transfer after some period of practice in another field.

It will be easier for you to learn how to become a fine PR practitioner having studied, for example, medicine, than it will be for you to become a doctor after majoring in public relations at college. If you decide to study for a bachelor's degree in public relations, or a closely related field such as journalism or communications, your second degree or course of study should be in an alternative field that will enhance your career potential – for example, international affairs, business administration, political science or languages of the countries in which you are interested. Such study will give you an edge in your career.

In contrast, if your first degree is in a field unrelated to communications, you should consider a master's degree program in public relations. Yes, such courses do exist, e.g. at Stirling University in the UK , in Barcelona and at various colleges in the USA. Your career prospects will not be damaged in any way – indeed they may be enhanced – if you choose to combine two complementary courses for both a bachelor's and master's degree and neither has public relations, journalism, or communications as a major.

There are many excellent short courses in communications technique and theory which, along with workplace learning, will build on your studies to equip you to be an excellent practitioner.

How you plan your career development once you have entered the world of business or government will be as important to your achievement of the profession's glittering prizes as your basic education. The person who aspires to reach the pinnacle in international public relations will need to be multi-talented, with wide experience: Educationally qualified, a skilled communicator, a thoughtful and calculating strategist, technologically proficient, multilingual, avidly interested in current affairs, knowledgeable about political affairs in many countries, respectful of a variety of customs and etiquette, and experienced in working in a number of countries, with a spell in general management.

■ Technological proficiency

The successful PR practitioner will be technologically proficient in three ways.

First, he himself will be sufficiently computer literate and competent in keyboard skills so as to be in regular communication within his own organization as well as with key audiences. In the extreme example, he should be self-reliant enough to be able to undertake practical communications initiatives from his own desktop, laptop or hand-held personal computer without the help of an assistant. This will mean a lifetime of learning new tricks.

Second, in order to make choices, he must have sufficient command of technological developments, and the advantages, disadvantages and prices of competing equipment and enhancements available to organizations as the infrastructure of their communications departments.

Third, this knowledge must extend to the way in which technological advances are constantly reshaping the media, shifting importance from one technique to another, so as to develop strategies and tactics that respond to these changes in good time.

Technophobes will go the way of the dinosaur.

■ Languages

Proficiency in more than your native language is a major advantage. It signals both your respect for and interest in people of other nations, in addition to allowing you to work more easily in a variety of environments. And this says nothing of the joy, stimulation and fun you will get from the access you will have to other literature and conversations. You will save time and cost in obtaining translations, and you will put interactions with your colleagues and audiences in other nations on a different and stronger footing.

However, a warning: do not imagine that a mere facility to speak foreign languages is sufficient to establish a worthwhile career in international public relations. I have known people with a knack for learning several languages who, sadly, had little of consequence to say in any of them, or were incapable of real communication. Better to learn the secrets of effective communications and practice them in one or two languages. And, in important business meetings – negotiating a contract, interviews with the media – always have a professional interpreter present. Executives who are highly competent but less than totally fluent in a foreign language can make embarrassing mistakes when they misinterpret the nuance of a word. The additional time taken for translation also helps you formulate a better answer.

■ Current affairs

As you will read elsewhere in this book, it is essential that you keep up with current affairs through regular reading and viewing of a selection of media. Only in this way will you be able to keep pace with the events that affect the lives of people in all the markets of importance to you and your organization. This reading program must involve publications from foreign countries.

I define current affairs as all important aspects of the life of any nation – politics, economics and business, arts, entertainment and sports.

■ Political affairs

Along with keeping abreast of current affairs, it is important that you familiarize yourself with the political structures in all key regions. Although ruling parties and their leaders may come and go (as your current affairs reading will show), the constitutions and political characteristics of many countries do not change. Even when seismic change has taken place, as has been the case in many of the countries of Eastern Europe, you should make it your business to know where power resides and where decisions of importance to your concern are made.

■ Customs and etiquette

Respect for the customs and etiquette of each distinct society, country, nation or religion is essential. Not only should these customs be learned, they should be practiced.

In the learning, you will often find the keys that open the door to improved communication, and that is your business. Without this knowledge, there can be no success, even for someone well qualified in all other respects.

■ International work experience

At a seminar of the Arthur W. Page Society entitled "Public Relations Leadership in 2001: Greater Importance, Greater Competition," Frank Vogl pointed out that "Globalization will impact every aspect of the PR Chief's work." Stressing that the communications function must reflect the new international approach apparent in so many major corporations, Vogl referred to an article in the *Wall Street Journal* on January 29, 1996, which said that "... the executive suite is going global. With nearly every industry targeting fast-growing foreign markets, more companies are requiring foreign experience for top management positions."

To illustrate its argument, the *Wall Street Journal* noted that, for example, Samir Gibara, president and CEO of Goodyear Tire & Rubber, had worked abroad for 27 of his 30 years with the company; Raymond Vialut, vice chairman of General Mills, was previously president and CEO of Kraft Jacobs Suchard in Switzerland; Michael Hawley, the president and CEO of Gillette, spent 20 of his 35 years with the corporation outside of the US; Harry Bowman reached the top at Outboard Marine after heading the European business of Whirlpool; and Lucio Noto, chairman and CEO of Mobil Oil, worked abroad for 17 of his 34 years with the corporation.

What's good for the CEO is equally essential for the global public relations practitioner. The top jobs of the future will surely be reserved for those who have worked in more than one market. This is confirmed by Peter Gummer, chairman of Shandwick, one of the world's largest international PR networks: "I am confident that the future of this company will be based on working in a global relationship with twenty or more major clients paying fees in the millions of dollars annually. The only people who will be able to offer counsel and service at the level required by such clients will be those who have multi market and multi disciplinary experience. Right now few of these exist. There are great opportunities for all who groom themselves by working in three or four different markets."

■ Switch places

Even if you plan to make your career in an agency or consultancy, a spell of two or three years working in-house at a corporation, government department or other institution will be valuable experience. It will give you special insight into the minds of your clients and the pressures they face within their own organizations. Some in-house PR executives are skeptical of the advice given by their external counselors because they suspect it is given without accountability for the outcome. Your advice will be more respected if your client knows that you have at one time stood in his shoes.

For the practitioner who will spend his working life within an organization, a period of agency experience can be valuable. But a period working in line management is even more useful and pays dividends later in policy and positioning debates; peers will recognize that the views being expressed are not purely based on theory. On-the-job experience was a key requirement for the most senior PR position in United Parcel Service. So in 1988, when Ken Sternad was selected based on his performance in the PR department ever since he had transferred from journalism in 1977, he was sent into general management as a district manager in Baltimore for two years. In this position, he had to deal with sales, vehicle maintenance, labor issues and union negotiations, pick-up and delivery scheduling – all the nuts and bolts of the business of UPS.

Now, he is head of PR in a company with annual sales of $23 billion, 338,000 employees and serving 200 countries around the world; his views are respected as coming from someone with a first-hand knowledge of the business and valued because he is a skilled communications expert.

It is increasingly unusual for PR practitioners to spend an entire career, or even a large proportion of their working lives, in a single organization. UPS is a singular corporation in many respects. But direct line management experience is immensely valuable in enlarging your professional capability.

■ Quick tip no. 1

Many organizations have severe budget constraints but desperately wish to communicate internationally. The costs involved in using several local agencies put a full-scale program out of reach. There are low-cost, short-cut alternatives for basic marketing and investor communications. PR Newswire and its affiliates and competitors offer attractive "packages" for news release distribution worldwide or to selected regions or specified countries. They will condense, translate and carry your news story on their wire. One snag: it is hard to check results and get feedback.

■ Quick tip no. 2

If your headquarters is located in a major city – your nation's capital or an economic center such as New York – make sure you identify the names of the foreign correspondents for international media who are resident there. You will find that all major publications and TV stations maintain a full-time correspondent or a "stringer". Get to know them because they will be assigned to cover your company's news and can act as a useful conduit into your worldwide markets. Lists are usually easy to get through the foreign correspondents clubs or from the local government information services which provide accreditation. In the USA, such lists are easy to get from media directories, municipal or police department accreditation offices, or by inquiring from local public relations clubs and societies.

CHAPTER 2

Corporate Reputation

A strong and positive corporate reputation is the holy grail of every public relations professional.

At Edelman Public Relations Worldwide, the management of corporate reputation is defined as, "The orchestration of discrete public relations initiatives designed to promote or protect the most important brand you own – your corporate reputation."

This reputation will be good or bad, strong or weak depending on the quality of strategic thinking, the management's commitment to achieving its stated goals, and the skill and energy with which all component programs are implemented and communicated.

Corporate reputation – or image, as advertising professionals prefer to term it – is based on how the company conducts or is perceived as conducting its business. A constellation of elements contributes to this reputation, as shown in the following diagram. Each element is discussed in other chapters of this book.

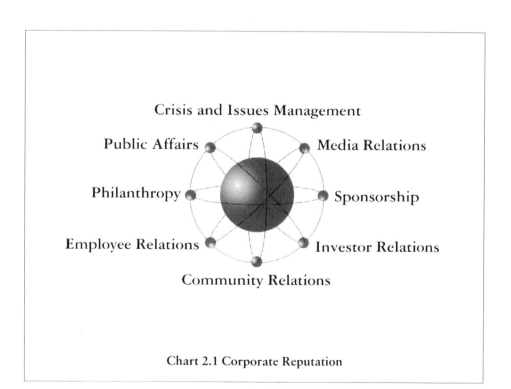

Chart 2.1 Corporate Reputation

When corporate reputation is secure, a flow of positive and tangible benefits accrues to the organization. And, it is an important shield in times of crisis.

Because businesses today operate in an environment of stress that often seems close to bursting into crisis, a carefully nurtured corporate reputation is all the more important.

Consider the market forces at play. Stock price performance has never been under such close and regular scrutiny, especially in the USA, where there is a quarterly disclosure of financial results by public companies. Chief executives are under extreme pressure to produce quarter after quarter of increasing profits and this militates against any venture and investment with a long-range pay-out. Corporate reputation is one such long-term investment.

Mergers and acquisitions across borders, often under hostile circumstances, are taking place at an accelerating pace, leaving many managements uneasy about an independent future and employees unsure their jobs will be safe under different ownership.

Even though many candidates for political office seek election on a platform of "less government" (with the promise that there will be less interference in industry and business), in reality the tide of legislation and regulation is on the increase – even if that paradoxically means de-regulation.

As corporations contend with globalization of their markets, their organizations and their competitors, there are enormous strains and changes with which to deal. Externally, the simultaneous fractionalization and concentration of traditional media and the growth of new media are new complexities facing public relations professionals.

In such a turbulent climate, a positive corporate reputation can play a vital role in ensuring an organization is on a solid footing. It will prove a powerful tool in what we might call "business climate stress management".

Following are some important examples of the benefits of a good corporate reputation.

■ Stock value

Shareholder value can be measurably improved. Corporate reputation and the confidence it inspires in investors will lead to a higher stock price for one company than for others that appear to be equal in all other respects but neglect the care of reputation.

Warren Buffet, chairman of Berkshire Hathaway, who has won legendary renown as a consistently successful investor, alluded to this phenomenon in a 1996 prospectus. With a touch of humor rare in such usually fact-filled and dry documents, he said he thought the stock in his investment company was really overvalued and he would not be a new buyer at that price. But he went on to say: "Berkshire believes that its reputation has added significantly to its value over the years. Berkshire further believes that its reputation, if it remains unimpaired, will produce substantial gains in the future as well."

Supporting that view is research data from Opinion Research Corporation (ORC), which conducts "Corperceptions", a periodic caravan survey of more than 4,000 business executives in several of the world's major markets. At the conclusion of its survey and analysis, "Corperceptions" gives each company a "Corporate Equity Rating", a score based on a number of criteria.

ORC CORPerceptions Criteria

1. Customer Focus
- Quality of products and service
- Value for $
- Responsiveness

2. Competitive Effectiveness
- Quality of Management
- Investment strategy/financial soundness
- Research and development focus

3. Market Leadership
- Vision
- Differentiation

4. Corporate Culture
- Social responsibility
- Ability to attract and retain employees
- Employee development

5. Communications
- Communicates effectively with all publics

Chart 2.2

ORC concludes that the better the corporate reputation, the higher the stock price. "There is a strong correlation between higher corporate equity ratings and higher price: earnings (P/E) ratios," says Dr. James Fink of ORC, illustrating the point with chart 2.3.

There is a large school of CEOs for whom the enhancement of shareholder value is the one and only goal. All other stakeholders are considered subsidiary. For these

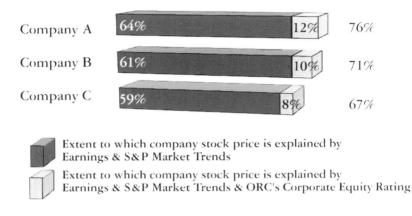

Company A 64% 12% 76%

Company B 61% 10% 71%

Company C 59% 8% 67%

Extent to which company stock price is explained by
Earnings & S&P Market Trends

Extent to which company stock price is explained by
Earnings & S&P Market Trends & ORC's Corporate Equity Rating

Chart 2.3 Corporate Reputation and the Stock Price

executives, the ORC Corperception data will be a convincing argument in favor of achieving a positive corporate reputation.

But a good stock price is just one of several important benefits. Moreover, present day realities unequivocally underline the need to satisfy the needs of certain key stakeholders if the investor is ever to see a good return.

■ Customers

Customers are more loyal to the products of companies with a good reputation. This is especially true when marketing communications make a strong connection between the company and its branded products or services. When corporate and product names are identical, as with Mobil, AT&T, Coca Cola, Visa and IBM, corporate and brand images are synonymous, making management of the reputation doubly important.

"If the perception of a company is negative, consumers will downgrade the quality of goods and services the company offers. If you have a positive reputation, it is easier to introduce new products because the customers get a guarantee of a certain quality of service with the name," says Lawrence Wortzel, professor of marketing at Boston University's School of Management.

Faith Popcorn, futurist and founder of the research organization Brain Reserve, predicts that consumers will increasingly be influenced in the products they buy by their feelings toward the companies that produce them.

■ Partners and allies

Corporate reputation is exceptionally influential when it comes to the partnerships and strategic alliances on which companies must rely for success in the increasingly complex, technology-driven and international world of business. The best suppliers, consultants, advertising agencies, potential joint-venturists, even PR agencies, prefer to establish partnerships and strategic alliances with companies of good reputation. The chances of a successful relationship are greater and the partner company helps improve its own reputation by association.

■ Employee morale and recruitment

Employee morale and commitment are generally much better at companies with a good corporate reputation, and this, in turn, usually leads to high productivity and good customer relations. Beyond existing employees, the reputation of an organization is a powerful factor in recruitment at all levels. Companies in industries that rely on technology, for example, must attract student stars to ensure that they maintain an innovative edge. A good reputation can win the honors graduates; a tarnished image will drive the best talent to the competition.

■ Government relations

A company with a solid reputation is much more likely than one held in low esteem to be able to influence the legislative or regulatory government decision-making process. This could affect millions in profits and create or eliminate jobs.

Consider one of the most competitive industries that exists today – economic development. In no area of business life is competition fiercer than in the attraction of investment, factories, infrastructure, all with the goal of creating jobs and wealth.

Governments of countries, states, counties, cities and towns vie with each other to entice companies to establish operations in their jurisdictions, offering a variety of blandishments that include free or cheap land, tax abatements, the establishment of schools, technical colleges and universities to educate the workforce, and the building of homes and other infrastructures for the company's employees.

South Carolina is said to have spent over $50,000 for each job created, when it won an intense competition to entice BMW to establish its first US automobile production plant in that state.

BMW's stellar reputation had helped it secure a superb deal. It could have chosen from many suitors. It had great bargaining power within the framework of electoral politics – the creation of jobs in a fine company is a guaranteed vote catcher.

■ Crisis shield

The value of a good corporate reputation and the penalties of a poor one are never more evident than in times of crisis. In fact, it is sad to say that it often takes a serious crisis to awaken certain agnostic corporate leaderships to the need for actions and communications geared to improving corporate reputation; it becomes apparent in time of crisis that a good reputation can be a shield.

John Garnett, prolific lecturer and pioneering leader of the Industrial Society, described a good reputation or image as providing a company "with a reservoir of good will", a concept he learned during his period as a manager in Imperial Chemical Industries (ICI). This reservoir of good will should be deep enough to draw on in times of drought or crisis, allowing the company to continue operating without undue harm until the crisis is resolved.

When a company with a good corporate reputation is confronted by a crisis or serious problem, it gets the benefit of the doubt from its important audiences who may well say, "This is a fine, well-managed company, with a solid record. There is probably no truth in the rumors/allegations. Even if there is, they will put things right and get back on track without undue damage."

In the same situation, a poorly regarded company will be assumed to be guilty from the outset. It will have to struggle to communicate its point of view, and its explanations will lack credibility. It will likely have to pay a higher cost for the experience.

The value of a reservoir of goodwill in time of crisis is pointedly described by Rebecca Madeira, vice president of public affairs of Pepsi Cola Company, following an incident in which a hoax was played on the company. News reports said someone had tampered with cans of Diet Pepsi and there were products on sale containing hypodermic syringes. Pepsi quickly defused public alarm with massive, forthright communications about the integrity of its manufacturing, underpinned by its corporate credibility. Ms. Madeira said, "Your reputation is your trade mark; it can be your biggest asset or your biggest liability. It is an asset because you can show the consumers how you've been able to make billions of cans safely, with quality and a taste you can trust, for the past 95 years."

■ The Strathclyde statement

Whether called corporate reputation, image or identity, this is the subject of lively study and debate in business and academic circles. Descriptions abound. The following summary, known as the "Strathclyde Statement", is the result of a collaborative effort on the parts of John Barlow, professor of marketing at Strathclyde University, Glasgow, Scotland, and Stephen Greyser, professor of marketing at the Harvard Business School.

"Corporate identity management is concerned with the conception, development and communication of an organization's mission, philosophy and ethos. Its orientation is strategic and is based on a company's values, cultures and behaviors.

"The management of corporate identity draws on many disciplines including strategic management, marketing, corporate communications, organizational behavior, public relations and design. It is different from traditional brand marketing directed towards household or business to business product purchases since it is concerned with all of an organization's stakeholders and the multi-faceted way in which an organization communicates. It is dynamic, not static, and is greatly affected by changes in the external environment.

"When well managed, an organization's identity results in loyalty from its diverse stakeholders. As such it can positively affect organizational performance, e.g. its ability to attract and retain customers, achieve strategic alliances, recruit executives and employees, be well positioned in financial markets, and strengthen internal staff identification with the firm."

CHAPTER 3

Corporate Reputation Management

With the value of a good corporate reputation clearly established, your task turns to the process of managing this key asset, on a global basis.

Reality and corporate reputation are inextricably linked. Not even the most skilled and seasoned PR professional can create and sustain a good reputation for a bad company. But at one time or another, most PR counselors are indeed asked to work this magic and some foolish practitioners believe they can do it.

In such cases, the role of the PR counselor or executive (a difficult one, admittedly) is to persuade management to change the reality by revising offensive policies and practices, and then to communicate these efforts so as to improve the reputation.

The previous chapter should be a useful tool in persuading management of the real benefits that will follow the establishment of a good reputation, turning it into a corporate "must" rather than a "nice to have".

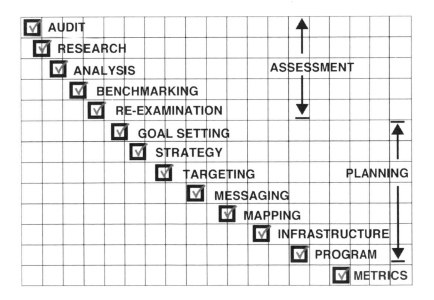

Chart 3.1 The Process

Your superiors and peers in management will be further encouraged if you adopt a methodical approach to the process of corporate reputation management. The process recommended has 13 steps, stretching from initial audit to measurement of achievement, as shown in chart 3.1.

The first five stages or steps in the corporate reputation management process are concerned with an assessment of the current situation in which the company finds itself.

■ 1. Audit

Start the process with an audit that should be largely internal.

- Collect and review as much existing data as you can about the company's ethos and way of doing business. It is possible, but unlikely in the case of most companies, that there are written statements on values, vision and mission. If they exist, get them into your data bank. Include corporate advertisements and even product advertisements to establish the promises that the company has made. Go back to the company's roots – examine the writings of the founders and others who have shaped the organization; examine the company history (if one exists) or what has been written elsewhere about them. All of this will give you a special insight into the evolution and character of the organization, a useful fundamental in the creation of its corporate identity and reputation.
- Review all current company communications tools – the annual report, newsletters and magazines, videos, website, etc.
- Survey the company's worldwide communications executives about what they view as critical issues. Include some non-PR personnel in the panel that receives your questionnaire.
- Interview a select number of senior executives in the company's principal markets around the world and in each of the main operating divisions, to assess the internal view of the company's reputation.
- Initiate a literature search (Lexis-Nexis or an equivalent database that is relevant to your company's field of activity) to establish how the firm has been portrayed recently in the media.

■ 2. Research

- Gather and consolidate all market and consumer research done by the various departments and operating divisions in your company. You will probably be surprised at the wealth of information that exists in various nooks and crannies, which can be useful in building up a composite picture of your organization's reputation. You may find market research that has been commissioned by the brands marketing people and investor attitude data that has been supplied to the investor relations director by the advertising departments of business magazines and by brokerage houses. You will probably also find research commissioned on behalf of trade associations in which your company has membership. You might be the first person who gathers all this data in one place, and, by comparing components

---

CORPORATE REPUTATION CRITERIA

Fortune Magazine
Quality of Management
Quality of products and services
Innovativeness
Long term investment value
Wise use of corporate assets
Ability to attract, develop and keep
talented people
Responsibility to the community and
environment

Far East Economic Review
Management has long term vision
High quality of services or products
Innovative in responding to customer needs
Financial soundness
Companies that others try to emulate

Chart 3.2

and cross referencing, you will be able to draw useful conclusions about the corporate reputation.

- Review the free research that is available to you. Analyst reports (financial and industry) should be obtained and studied. Look especially carefully at the annual "report card" issues of the principal newspapers and magazines. For purposes of monitoring corporate reputation, the edition of *Fortune* on "Most Admired Companies in the USA" is required reading, as is the equivalent issue of the *Far East Economic Review*. The attributes considered in each survey are quite similar and as useful a checklist as any that exists for corporate reputation managers.

- Check the availability of ready-made historical research, which might be relatively inexpensive to access. If your company is a leader in its field, research material on it was quite likely included in cooperative or caravan studies conducted by organizations such as Opinion Research Corporation (ORC), Yankelovich, Market Opinion Research International (MORI), or Penn & Schoen, seeking to provide their clients with comparative data. A call to these companies and others in your area could yield a pleasant surprise – the existence of data at a substantial saving of time and money.

- If there is no existing research, consider commissioning custom-made research or subscribing to the regular co-op or caravan studies conducted by reputable organizations. Give special consideration to MORI in the UK and Yankelovich or Penn & Schoen in the USA, because they have demonstrated an ability to get responses from usually impenetrable groups of law makers, government officials, academics and the media. Similar organizations exist in many other countries, allowing you to build up a picture of your company in all your key regions. You are likely to find a widely differing reputation from market to market.

■ 3. Analysis

- Distill the findings of the mass of data that you have collected into a coherent report.

- Check the regional and national variations in your corporate reputation. This will give you pointers as to where you must focus your efforts.
- Write a short description of the company as it is perceived, based on what you have found out. Later, you will write a similar description of the company as you would like people to see it. Your challenge will be to develop strategies and programs that will progressively move perceptions from the present reality to the goal you set.

■ 4. Benchmarking

Yours is not the first organization to have set off down this path. Others have done so and have achieved complete or partial success. You can learn by their experience. The process is known as benchmarking.

- Make a list of up to 20 companies you most admire and wish to emulate. A majority should be operating in the same business sector as your own company. The others should have some relevance, and all should be operating on an international basis. Not all the companies you approach to participate in the benchmarking will agree to do it, which is why an initial list of 20 was suggested. Ten participants will be sufficient to provide you with information that will be invaluable in guiding you in the planning and executional stages that are to follow. Develop carefully thought-out questions that are specific enough to elicit concrete answers about how other companies enhanced or protected their reputations. These questions will initially be in the form of a written questionnaire. Personal interviews will follow to drill deeper; these may be done on a visit or by phone.
- From the benchmarking, you will be able to determine which are best practices for the achievement of the corporate reputation you are seeking for your organization.
- The rule of benchmarking is that participants get a "return on investment" by receiving a copy of your executive summary of the exercise. Without divulging the names of participating companies, provide a short description of each one.

■ 5. Re-examination

You are now at the end of the assessment stage. It's time to re-examine and summarize the data that has been collected so far.

You may also decide to give an update to your management and colleagues in the corporate communications function. You will need their input and ideas in the planning and executional stages to come. In this re-examination, there are two important tasks.

- Summarize your findings so far.
- Undertake an analysis of your company's principal strengths, weaknesses, opportunities and threats, popularly known as a SWOT Analysis. Involve colleagues drawn from the communications function in your principal geographies and divisions. The analysis will provide you with a useful reputation balance sheet.

Your charter, of course, will be to build on and communicate the strengths, eliminate the weaknesses, seize the opportunities and inoculate against the threats.

■ 6. Goal setting

- If your assessment phase indicates that your company is heavily handicapped in terms of its reputation, you will need to consider phasing your goals to make their attainment a realistic possibility. This can be done by grouping your goals under two or three headings: short, medium and long term.
- Although goals should be broad and aspirational, at the same time they must be subject to measurement. So it is important to be specific as well. Eventually, when you come to the evaluation stage in the process, you must be able to measure whether you have achieved your goals or not. So rather than writing a woolly statement such as, "To improve our company's corporate reputation dramatically," write, "To ensure that our company becomes the most admired in its industry sector in the *Fortune/Far East Economic Review* annual survey." If you subscribe to Opinion Research Corporation's corporate reputation caravan study, your goal could be, "To increase our company's corporate equity rating by one full percentage point in the next two years and by two points in the next four years."
- It is quite acceptable to state a single, overriding objective, as just illustrated, with subsidiary goals set against each important audience or stakeholder group – investors, employees, customers, government, and so on.

■ 7. Strategy

- Outline your strategies in the same way that you have structured your goals. Make sure not to confuse strategies with tactics – a common mistake. Here is an easy way to distinguish: Goal/Objective = Where I want to get to. Strategy = Overall, how I get there. Tactics = Specifically what I have to do to get there.
- You must create different strategies for different markets around the world. Your research and analysis will have shown you widely differing perceptions of your company in the principal countries in which you do business. When United Parcel Service decided to embark on building a global infrastructure in 1988, it was already the world's largest package delivery company, based on its size in the three markets it served through its own resources: the USA, Canada and Germany. In the USA, the company was, literally, part of the landscape with its 120,000 delivery vehicles and 300,000 employees in their brown uniforms. Research surveys in America gave UPS a 100 per cent awareness rating. Still, the company knew that it had to make structural changes internally and alter perceptions among its customers and other stakeholders to keep its leadership position in that market. In the "new" markets of Europe and Asia, UPS was completely unknown. The challenge was to introduce the company there as a strong alternative to entrenched competitors. In Canada and Germany, there was a dual task of gaining wider recognition of the name UPS and reshaping some perceptions that had formed in

these markets. Different strategies were devised for each region, but all were geared to meet the overarching goal.

■ 8. Messaging

- Go back to Step 3, Analysis, and review the short statement you wrote to describe the reputation of your company as you feel it stands now. Prepare a new statement that reflects the company as you would like it to be seen at the culmination of this process. In addition to its role in message development, the new statement is necessary in the next step, Mapping.
- Synthesize the key messages that will become the mantra of all those empowered to act as spokesmen for the company. The messages will be the building blocks for creating a new perception of the company. Divide the messages into those that are global and overarching and those that have special importance in specific countries. Repetition of the messages by spokespersons will allow them to penetrate the consciousness of stakeholders and other audiences you seek to influence, and you should not let up.

■ 9. Mapping

- Translate your descriptions of your company's reputation now and as you would like it to be into a road map, with a starting point and a destination. This will help you track progress.
- Make individual maps for each area of reputation which you believe needs to be changed. For example, research may have shown that your company has especially weak scores for its attitude toward the environment and pollution, and trails its competitors in this regard. Plot the environmental issues map with as much specific detail as you can, including your competitors, as illustrated in chart 3.3.
- Data you receive from ORC will be mappable, as will the information you glean from generally available studies such as the "most admired" lists that appear in various publications. If you subscribe to MORI, you will receive this data already mapped in convenient form.
- In the map covering a company's "overall reputation" (Chart 3.4), I have shown the curve rising first on the awareness axis on the basis that it is sometimes easier to gain awareness and a correct perception of a company at the same time than it is to change entrenched impressions. There is an opposing view which holds that you must change perceptions with those who claim to know you before starting on the missionary work of increasing awareness.
- The worst starting position on reputation maps is at the top left of the upper quadrant. This is the place for a company that everybody knows ... and hates, with the awesome challenge of having to change everybody's current perception.

■ 10. Infrastructure

Make sure you create the right departmental infrastructure to meet your goals. Alternatives are more fully described in chapter 12.

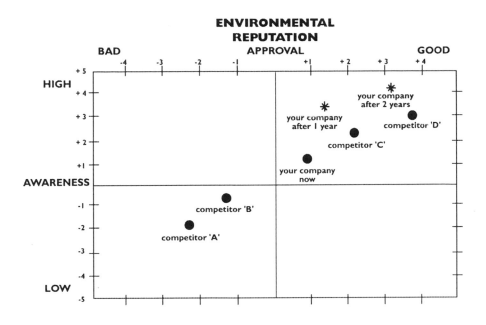

Chart 3.3

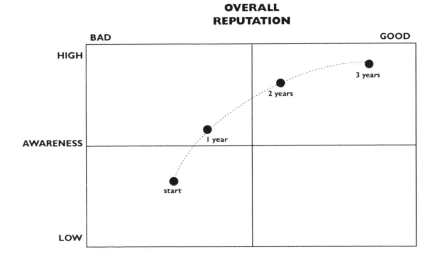

Chart 3.4

■ 11. Program

With your research and planning completed, you must now develop and implement the program that will move your company along the road toward its goal.

* Develop a memorable and inspiring creative concept, which symbolizes and encapsulates the reputation you seek for your company – a flag around which all your allies can rally. This concept or theme should be of a kind that can infuse all the action programs you undertake, binding them together.
* Develop your action plan – or plans. Do not start with a piece of white paper or a blank computer screen. Use checklists of all the possible tactics available to you and pick those that are useful, while rejecting those that are not relevant. Only when you have screened all known techniques, should you start thinking about completely original techniques that might be developed to meet your particular set of circumstances. Here is a fairly comprehensive public relations toolbox which can be built into core programs for implementation by units of your organization around the world:

Press conferences, editorial briefings
Press kits, fact sheets, photographs, backgrounders, news releases
Website
CDrom
Face-to-face meetings, presentation decks
Position papers, white papers
Op-eds
By-lined articles
Charts, graphs
VNRs, b-roll
Annual reports
Spokespersons, speakers platforms, publicity tours
Familiarization tours
Seminars, workshops
Surveys and polls
Event sponsorships
Charity tie-ins

* Develop country-specific and regional programs with your national PR directors.

■ 12. Measurement

Your work will have been wasted – and your own job will be in jeopardy – if you cannot demonstrate that you have achieved success in meeting your goals. At the outset of the process, establish with your superiors how the work will be judged. If you have businesslike yardsticks for measurement, your proposals will most likely be accepted. If not, you will almost certainly have arbitrary criteria established to judge your performance, by people who do not have a close understanding of what is and is not possible in the world of communications.

- You started with research. Continue, by monitoring your progress periodically to see if you are on track.
- Check if you have met your goals in the "most admired" company ratings produced by the leading business magazines.
- Re-audit your internal audiences to check how your colleagues feel the company is doing.
- Conduct an annual Critical Issues Analysis to see which issues you have managed to defuse and control, and which are growing in importance. (See chapter 8, Issues Identification and Management.)
- Conduct face-to-face interviews with key influencer groups.
- Read your road map. Based on composite research findings, check how far you have traveled toward your destination of the reputation you desire.
- Check that your stock price is at the desired P/E ratio.

■ 13. Targeting

The fact that this is one of the final steps in the process does not diminish its importance. Effective targeting will ensure economy of effort and budget. More important, it will ensure that you succeed in improving your reputation among those audiences that matter most to your organization's success.

- Start by listing all your stakeholders and audiences. Then list all those who exert a major influence on the attitudes of those in the first part of the list.
- You may list media as an audience. While media is an audience in its own right, it is even more important as a interlocutor with key influencers and decision makers, and as multiplier with broader consumer audiences.
- Prioritize your targets by general category, so that if budgets and resources are limited, you concentrate on those audiences that are most important.
- Prioritize within each general category. For example, not all customers are equal; not all influencers of governmental law-making are equal. Classify your targets into three levels of importance: A, B and C. Most attention and budget should be focused on the A list.
- Target by region and country of importance to your organization.
- Use the public databases that are available to you to build your target lists. You should also maintain your own regularly updated master database. Note on it each contact made by letter, mailing, phone call or meeting.

The management of the corporate reputation of a major organization is the challenge that most practitioners of PR aspire to as they reach the zenith of their careers. The task carries with it great responsibilities. It also draws on a wide range of skills and experience in the different public relations specialties.

CHAPTER 4

The Global Voice

Becoming a global corporation requires speaking with a global voice. This is not so easy as it sounds, and most companies find it difficult to establish the right messages and the right tone in which to express them. At this writing, there are no more than a handful of corporations with a commitment to becoming global in the fullest sense – Ford Motor, GE, IBM, Coca Cola and VISA are a few examples on this very short list. Nor are there many organizations that are truly multinational – the stage of development that immediately precedes the state of being global. Many corporations that believe they are multinational are really regional or super-regional, in the sense that they are well established in more than one region but fall short of being worldwide, or global, in their activities. Moreover, many are really national corporations that have expanded and added appendages in other countries, whose needs and views are not of any significance in the decision-making process.

■ Survival of concept

It will be interesting to see if the concept of the global corporation survives into the next century. To do so, it will have to overcome some powerful forces of economic nationalism and protectionism, as well as the internal pressure in many corporations, which together work to break up globalism into smaller pieces – either by geography or by the various lines of business in which they are engaged.

It will not be easy for most corporations, however big they are, to become truly global. This would mean a revolution in thinking which some will argue is against human nature. It means abandoning the enterprise's national identity, origins, center of gravity and community commitment, at least to a certain extent.

When hard decisions have to be made, say on the matter of selective plant closures in an economic downturn, the global corporation should, in theory, make its choices based on economic imperatives, even to the extent of closing facilities at the heart of its original home office. Sentiment, lobbying, industrial and political unrest can often be powerful factors in changing the best plan on paper into one that stands the best chance of being implemented.

■ Balance

One of the most challenging problems facing today's business leaders is finding the right balance between the devolution of power to so-called autonomous units within a corporation and the exercise of power and decision making at the world headquarters, wherever that might be.

Today's fashion leans heavily toward a highly decentralized approach, with a large part of decision making placed in the hands of managers of national subsidiary companies so as to encourage a high degree of nimbleness and relevance, market by market.

Empowerment is a very fashionable word. By applying it to individuals at every level in the company, top management hopes to achieve the best possible performance from each person, unit, country and region. The aggregate will automatically ensure success for the corporate entity as a whole.

The decentralized model also makes it easy for corporations to establish uncomplicated and clear-cut criteria for success and, in turn, compensation and incentive packages for key managers. The best get promoted and the weak get weeded out.

Among the positive advantages of this system, there is another, less often mentioned defensive benefit. When things go wrong, central managements believe they might be able first to contain the problem at the local level without any bad effect on the main body of the enterprise; and if containment is not possible, the offending unit can be blamed for not adhering to corporate policy and the management can be changed before too much harm is done.

This is sometimes referred to as the "submarine principle". The naval submarine is built with up to eight water-tight compartments so that it can survive a hit on any one or two of them by enemy torpedoes.

■ Purpose

With global corporations still in the embryonic stage and the majority of multinationals operating in a highly decentralized manner, what is the purpose and role of a "global voice"?

A "global voice" is the subject of considerable study and attention by many of the world's finest corporations, even though the subject might be disguised under a host of other names, depending on the alma mater of the CEO or the dialectic jargon of the company. "One voice", "single voice", "key messages" and "must airs" are examples.

These corporations have recognized that a global voice is not optional nowadays; it is a corporate necessity.

Nor is it something that is only of concern for the global corporation; it is a vital necessity for every company that is engaged in international business, even if it operates in a highly decentralized way in other respects.

There are several reasons why this should be.

■ Media technology

The first and most compelling reason is the impact of technology on globalization of the media. The CNN coverage of Desert Storm was seen live by nearly every country in the world. This dramatically brought home what had been reality for some time since the advent of satellite TV: it is no longer possible to have substantially different messages for different markets or audiences. (I say substantially because the same technology also allows the opportunity to develop micromessaging to very small specialist audiences.)

Now, when referring to the media, it is necessary to include the Internet and all its various services, which are accessible by anyone, anywhere, at any time. Although, as the use of this medium grows and new service providers enter the market, it will be possible for corporations to depict themselves on home pages in a variety of forms and languages for different audiences, it will still be possible for the Internet surfer to access the basic portrait of the corporation from his PC in France, the UK, Ukraine, China or the Philippines.

The potency of the Internet as a global voice in its own right was amply demonstrated in the celebrated 1995 case of the faulty Pentium chip. A single complaint about the chip was aired on the Internet and built a crescendo of customer comments that the manufacturer, Intel Corporation, initially dismissed in quite a cavalier fashion. It ended with Intel offering to replace the Pentium chip for any PC owner who applied, a gesture with a possible price tag in the region of $450 million.

■ Scrutiny

Increased scrutiny of the words and actions of corporations is another reason for a global voice. Governments, consumer protection organizations, nongovernmental organizations (NGOs) and pressure groups of all kinds are making it their business to discover inconsistencies in multinational concerns. It is now far too dangerous to allow the corporate position to be articulated by local company officials without adequate guidance – or even direction, in some cases – from company headquarters. There are many examples of sister companies in different countries, subsidiaries of the same parent corporation, that have been found to subscribe to apparently contradictory philosophies and procedures. There are plenty of official and unofficial watchdogs ready to point out such anomalies to the public and hold the corporation up to ridicule with subsequent damage to its image and its credibility.

Among the predators who are happy to discover different standards (and explanations) within a single corporation are "venture lawyers" and, of course, the company's competitors in the marketplace.

For the lawyers, any hint of dissembling can open up financially rewarding opportunities for litigation in certain societies, such as America. Nor are these litigious activities any longer contained within national borders. One of the least instructive and most unpleasant sights in the immediate aftermath of the Bhopal disaster in India and after the downing of Pan Am 103 at Lockerbie in Scotland was the large number of American trial lawyers trawling among the victims for clients to represent in the US as well as the local courts.

For the competitors, such misadventures can be used as weapons with which to damage the rival company's reputation and sales for their own advantage. Few corporations in today's fiercely combative marketplace could resist the opportunity to take advantage of any misstep on the part of a competitor.

■ Benefits

If the threats were not enough to make the case for a "global voice", then the benefits that flow from a well-articulated and disseminated "global voice" should tip the balance.

It can be argued that it is the more decentralized multinational corporations that stand to benefit most. It is here, rather than in the old-fashioned, highly centralized or newer global corporations, that there is found a degree of local anarchy that can result in differing corporate cultures, policies and, therefore, messages being communicated. For such decentralized corporations, a single voice is of great importance in today's global village. But more often than not, they sound more like the tower of Babel.

In an ideal world, the corporate or global voice should be descriptive of the reality. "The truth, well told" is an old advertising adage that might be appropriately applied to a well-executed global-voice concept for a company that strives for and achieves uniform excellence worldwide in every aspect of its business – in product quality, customer service, research and development, human relations, community relations.

The achievement of excellence, however, is not easy and takes steely resolve and time. For many companies, taking the first steps in this quest to establish a global voice can serve a different and valuable purpose – as a catalyst in the process of defining "the reality".

■ Mission statement

The precursor of any effective global-voice policy is the creation and adoption of a mission or vision statement that simply articulates the purpose and business of the enterprise: the corporate credo should be the guidelight for every executive and member of the company in whichever division or part of the world they may be.

Many sizable corporations still operate without the corporate mission being defined in this way. In a survey of 100 international companies conducted jointly by Edelman Public Relations Worldwide, Northwestern University and Opinion Research Corporation, 42 per cent had no corporate values system, 75 per cent of companies said they had no formalized mission/vision statement and 42 per cent even worked without a written public relations plan. So it is not surprising that the subsequent development in more detail of such a corporation's viewpoint on various components of its mission should be inconsistent and inadequate. If the foundation is faulty, the building will crumble.

Assuming that the first step – the writing and adoption of a mission statement – has taken place, here are the further steps that should be taken in the development of a Corporate Global Voice.

■ Key messages

The next step should be to develop more fully into key phrases or messages the main elements of the company's policy on important topics. These are most likely to include comments about production processes, enhancements of shareholder values, policies toward employee development, commitment to product quality and excellence in many facets of day-to-day operations – in fact, all the things the company would like to say about itself to a benign reporter or government official making inquiries.

But an effective global voice must go much further and be able to articulate the company viewpoint on a range of external issues that might be raised regarding how the company's actions affect society in various ways.

■ Issues analysis

The identification of these issues is best undertaken by a systematic process of analysis, which is described in more detail in chapter 8. In essence, it involves surveying members of the communications and other staff in each of the company's various geographic locations and lines of business, and cross-referencing the data received with that easily obtainable from various opinion research organizations that regularly track public opinion. Even careful reading of the media and use of data-retrieval systems can freely elicit public-attitude data of a general kind that is helpful in this process.

From this process will emerge a list (upward of 50 topics is not unusual) of issues on which the company will need to formulate a brief position. A few, between six and ten, are likely to emerge as issues in most major markets and will require significant effort in preparing a global voice.

For chemical companies, these are likely to touch on pollution, use of nonreplaceable fossil fuels, harmful effects when ingested, use of animals in testing of products, the disposal of waste and the possibility of explosions or environmental disasters.

For credit card companies, the issues of fraud, privacy, interest rates on outstanding balances and encouragement of use of credit by young people who have little chance to make payments are just a few of the universal problems that require uniform explanations and positions.

For tobacco, liquor and confectionery companies, all under varying degrees of control of distribution or advertising in many countries, there are a host of issues requiring global answers to obvious health-related questions.

The same is true of every company engaging in an international way of business, whatever its field (or fields) of endeavor may be.

■ Updating

Once the Global Voice policy has been started, it must be continued and constantly updated and refreshed. A periodic survey should be conducted to reprioritize the issues. It is almost certain that many will have receded in importance and others will have become more critical than ever. New concerns may be identified that have to be addressed for the first time, and old concerns may re-emerge in new ways.

CHAPTER 5

Think Global, Act Local

There is not likely to be a phrase you will hear in your career in public relations as often as "think global, act local." It is used to encourage international marketers and communicators to adapt their products or messages to be accepted in a variety of local communities around a region or around the world. The idea is that a good product, service or communications strategy can achieve global success as long as it is customized to meet local tastes.

A culinary equivalent might be a steak. An excellent piece of beef is described as tender, succulent and full of flavor. But, depending on where you are, some might prefer it rare or well done; grilled, fried or baked; plain or with bordelaise sauce, pepper sauce or forestiere. Without suitable adaptation, success will be elusive. When prepared for the regional palate, however, a fine piece of beef is likely to please.

But what about the fact that huge numbers of the world's people honor the cow and are offended by the notion that beef cattle are raised to end up on the dining table? Millions more are vegetarians. So mere customization, after all, is insufficient.

■ Post World War II

The internationalization of business in the post-World War II period and the parallel development of public relations have operated on this principle, which is generally seen as a refinement of the initial attempts by major corporations – mostly based in America in the early years – to export products or manufacture them locally, without any deviation from the products sold in the home country. This was: "Think global, act global."

It took a series of failures to achieve market penetration before businesses that were thinking global started acting local. Textbooks are full of examples of adaptations that had to be made to recover from these early reverses.

Manufacturers of home appliances had to learn that houses in Britain and many other countries in Europe were much smaller than in America, and the tiny kitchens could not accommodate the American standard size of refrigerator. Nor were houses built with basements in which the typical, large American washing machines could be installed. They, too, had to fit into the small kitchen alongside the refrigerator. This led quickly to miniaturization and local manufacture. The sizes and features of motor cars, which differ widely from continent to continent and country to country, are other well-known examples.

Hand in hand with the early attempts to think global, act global in product marketing went the efforts of corporate advertising and public relations departments. In the first wave, highly centralized communications were the order of the day. The advertisement that was created for placement in the *Cincinnati Enquirer* would have to suffice for the *Northampton Evening Telegraph* or the *South China Morning Post*, without alteration of a word or change of spelling.

The news releases written for and sent to city newspapers, whether the *New York Times* or the *San Francisco Examiner*, were also sent to the *Brighton Argus*, the *Sydney Morning Herald* and the *Daily Record* in Glasgow, sometimes without a local contact name and address. Even more remarkably, the same English-language communications were sent to media in France, Germany and elsewhere, in the naive hope that they would be welcomed, understood and published.

Ultimately, ads were adapted for individual markets and in some cases were even recreated to combat local competitors or to deal with specific local conditions, on the basis of accumulated experience and market research. Public relations was swift to adjust and start "acting local". Editors, journalists, opinion leaders, politicians, academics, pressure groups and civil servants are quick to voice opinions and they are the audiences or interlocutors for most public relations professionals. They have little time for catch-all communications that were obviously prepared for another audience in another country. At best, such efforts were disregarded and had no effect. At worst, they caused offense, creating a negative impression of the sender.

■ Early internationalists

The early internationalists were quick to learn. They employed public relations professionals, mostly recruited from the ranks of journalism, onto their staffs or into the emerging roster of consultancies and agencies that began to sprout up in London. Britain was well ahead of the other countries of Europe in this development, in large part because it was the primary location of the European headquarters of the major American companies.

This cadre of communicators had the dual function of educating their foreign "parents" in the customs, culture, sociology, politics and media of the local market, and reworking communications strategies and messages for local consumption. In the 1950s and 1960s, the development of public relations in Britain, at least, was as an adjunct to advertising although there were some very successful and prominent independent firms and individuals who specialized in public affairs. The largest consultancies were initially departments and, later, autonomous divisions of advertising agencies. It was late in the 1960s when the independent public relations consultancies began to rise to preeminence – until many of them were themselves acquired by ad agencies. One rationale for such acquisitions was that the major multinational clients of these agencies could be offered "the whole egg" (as Young & Rubicam described it). This meant one-stop shopping for clients, with integrated, or at least "bundled", services offered by advertising, research, sales promotion and public relations functions. Each agency had its own description of such combined marketing and communications support services. At Ogilvy & Mather the concept was described as "orchestration": the client acted as the maestro, or conductor, of several instruments of marketing, bringing them all together in perfect timing, pitch and harmony.

The "think global" concept did not receive a warm welcome in every new market. The relentless rise of the multinational corporation posed a series of threats or, at least, perceived threats, to local communities in Europe and elsewhere. People and politicians became alarmed at what they felt was a creeping commercial colonization. From 1950 until 1985, the tension felt in Europe about the success of American corporations in foreign markets was matched by the alarm of Americans over Japanese inroads into the US automobile market, and in electronics, real estate and the entertainment industries in the 1980s and 1990s. To a lesser extent, America reacted with concern over foreign investment in US business and the consequences for the US economy. European companies, predominantly from Britain and Switzerland, were buying their way into ownership of US companies, many of them symbolic of the "American Dream".

The publication in France of Jean-Jacques Servan Schreiber's book, *Le Defi Americain*, signaled the peak of European reaction to the seeming takeover of the European industrial infrastructure by US-based multinationals, and the consequential impact on social, educational and family structures. Schreiber, a prominent French journalist, described the damaging effect he felt that American capitalist colonization had had in France and painted a scary picture of the future. He urged that the phenomenon be resisted at all costs. Among the effects was renewed emphasis on building the European Economic Community, now the EU, as a counterbalance.

On the other side, the less farsighted and thoughtful of the multinational companies reviewed their policies and joined the well-managed companies that had already adopted "act local" policies.

■ "Act local" benefits

Not only were these policies proven to be a useful defense against criticism of commercial imperialism, but they also turned out to have a variety of significant positive benefits. Some of the best new inventions and marketing concepts came from foreign employees in overseas units. Some overseas units outperformed the domestic operations when measured by growth and return on investment. And excellent young managers were being developed, many of whom ended up in key positions at the head office or went on to establish new subsidiaries in new markets.

And what did acting local involve? In essence, it meant that foreign-owned companies started acting as if they were members of the local communities in which they developed, made and sold their products, rather than as foreign invaders.

In actions, they sought to invest in production facilities and, in certain cases, even in research and development laboratories. They participated in local activities and increasingly became involved in education, and even the church.

■ PR actions

From a public relations or communications standpoint, these companies sought to make sure that the world was aware of their local involvement. They were at pains to be seen and accepted as local citizens rather than transient marauders who come, take what they want and then abandon the locality, rather like the Vikings.

The companies primarily publicized their actions to support the local community and host country. News releases and press conferences would put the spotlight on local acts: investment in new production facilities that would increase job opportunities, announcements of promotions and transfers of local executives, production records, funding of local charities, participation in local festivals, donations to schools and colleges, foreign earnings generated by exports from the unit, inventions or advances inspired by the local work force.

Some of the most serious examples of this full-blooded attempt to "act local" and to be recognized for doing so can be seen in the advertisements of many companies, notably IBM, which depicted individual nationals from several countries in each ad. The effect of the whole was to suggest that this huge multinational was, in fact, the federal headquarters of a number of independent and autonomous national entities run by locals. PR activities echoed this theme.

It certainly had its effect.

While foreign computer and technology corporations are forbidden by law from bidding for many US defense and other government contracts, IBM's lobbyists managed to get IBM/Europe classified as a European company, by virtue of its thousands of European employees, exports and importance to the European economies, so that it could bid for official contracts of the European Economic Community.

■ Think local

Yet the question remains: Does not the phrase "think global, act local" reflect an imperialistic economic attitude? At worst, it conjures up a colonial ambition in which the locals are satisfied with the offer of various beads and baubles, becoming pawns in a grand plan. Mostly, of course, it is common sense for executives cutting their teeth in the international business world and is sound as far as it goes.

But it may be much more effective – certainly for PR people and other communicators – to reverse the advice and "Think local, act global". This may seem just tinkering with words ("you end doing the same things, anyway"), but I beg to differ.

Tip O'Neill, the longtime Speaker of the US House of Representatives, is credited with saying, "All politics is local". He was right. In a democracy, ultimate power rests with the voter who might be moved by leadership and a dramatically articulated vision but most often has to make judgments based on local input and a "what's in it for me" attitude.

By "thinking local", you can reach a level of understanding of the mind-set of each group of people with whom you must communicate that will make your dialogue much more successful. By "acting local", you can pose but may never achieve the required level of understanding to succeed and be accepted as local.

If you are able to "think local", or at least listen to and understand the advice of those who can, you will stand a much better chance of being able to put your case in terms that are comprehensible by and convincing to your local audience. Thinking local means much, much more than translating, customizing and even localizing news releases and other communications.

It means understanding local history, customs, rituals, taboos and prejudices. It means knowing what does and does not make news. It means respecting that a local community's perception, motivation or priority represents a different outlook. It means patience.

Success in thinking local brings its own problems, however, the greatest of which is retaining loyalty to the global vision and mission of the organization. It can be a challenge to step from thinking local to acting global, when so often the two seem to be at odds with each other. This is where corporate resolve and commitment, tempered by compromise, are of the greatest importance.

■ Backlash

Japanese business leaders had to learn to think local before they could even act local.

As they achieved increasing success in penetrating the US market with sales of automobiles and electronics – as well as a host of other items – they felt the backlash of public opinion from Americans, who believed their jobs and way of life were under threat by a country that had been their recent enemy. In the next phase of Japanese globalization, the new-found wealth of the Japanese came back to be reinvested in America, in local manufacture or assembly of products, as well as in the purchase of prime real estate.

At the outset, the Japanese appeared not to be good corporate citizens in their many locations, something that caused concern back at headquarters. Efforts were made to find the reasons and put matters right. The firms recognized that they had to *learn* how to think local before they could act local.

■ Corporate philanthropy

Among the many differences between American and Japanese commercial practices, human relations, manufacturing procedures and cultures, one phenomenon became apparent: the Japanese were completely ignorant of the concept of volunteerism, community service and charitable giving that is such an integral part of American business life. Social responsibility in Japan manifests itself in other ways, such as provision of lifetime employment. Japanese corporations did not routinely make charitable donations or support community initiatives, seeing them as the responsibility of national or local government. What's more, the Japanese also are not accustomed to the private raising of large sums of money following natural disasters. Foreigners did this after the 1994 Kyoto earthquake, to help with the costs of medical care and repair to the infrastructure. The Japanese have no system for accepting and using such contributions, which, in turn, makes them appear insensitive and arrogant. Nevertheless, the Japanese were determined to understand what it takes to be a good citizen in their adopted country, and at the top of the list was the topic of corporate philanthropy, not to be confused with cause-related marketing.

This led to the creation of a specialized branch of consulting in which individuals and firms would advise Asian companies eager to understand this concept as applied in the United States. Some of these consultants could even act as the selectors of the beneficiaries of this corporate philanthropy on a local basis, which might be anything from the construction of a community swimming pool to the addition of a new wing to the library or uniforms for the marching band.

■ Understanding other cultures

If it has been hard for Asian managers and communicators to comprehend the European and American way, it was equally so for the Western executive to understand – and respect – the ways and customs of the Asian markets he sought to conquer.

Newcomers to the area of greater China, for example, are amused by and often deride the vital importance of *feng shui*. And the *feng shui* man is likely to be one of their first encounters, for he is the person who dictates – yes, dictates – the angle and placement of the reception desk, as well as the layout of the office or factory that is being rented or built. This skill is based on a combination of magical arts, including astrology, rather than his Western cousins' degrees in environmental engineering, ergonomics and industrial psychology.

Many Western companies have paid a heavy price with their local staff, suppliers and customers for ignoring the *feng shui* man, or for treating him as a figure of fun. It is a rare Chinese business leader – including any one of the scores of Hong Kong billionaires – who would inaugurate new premises without having taken the advice of the *feng shui* expert. Even such a wealthy person will meekly agree to the office allocated to him and will place his desk at the angle recommended.

McDonald's – a model of globalization – has had its own encounters with local custom. Its international expansion during a quarter of a century has evolved into a system that allows for a great deal of local modification of menu items, to appeal to local tastes, and even terminology. In Australia, signs at roadside read "MACCA's – 5KM ON RIGHT".

Such liberties were unthinkable in the 1980s. When the first McDonald's restaurant was opened in Kuala Lumpur, Malaysia, in 1983, questions were raised in the company's Chicago headquarters, and then incredulity at the answers, regarding an item that appeared on the invoice for the inaugural press and opinion-leader event: "Bomo Man M$500."

Who was this Bomo Man?

The Bomo Man, came the answer, is a key figure at every important, outdoor public event in Malaysia. He is a "rain man", but, unlike the better known rainmakers in the West, he performs a dance and casts spells to ensure that rain stays away during celebrations. McDonald's grand opening had taken place in perfect weather, thanks to the Bomo Man, the accounting people were told. The Malaysian partners of McDonald's had a hard time understanding what kind of ignorance could prompt the questions from Chicago. It was just as hard for the Midwest executives to believe they were looking at a valid expense.

Nonetheless, they paid the M$500.

CHAPTER 6

The Barriers

It is a characteristic of many public relations people to be paranoid, introspective, and doubting. A few even add a measure of self pity.

Far too many people in public relations are convinced that they practice a profession that is in low esteem and that growth is impeded. They feel relegated to a lower caste of management in their companies.

The facts prove differently. Public relations is fast growing. One need only look at those countries which have recorded the fees of the leading public relations agencies/consultancies over several years. In the USA, the combined fees of the top ten agencies recorded in the O'Dwyer rankings have grown from $100,000,000 in 1976 to $1,547,000,000 in 1996. In the UK, the *PR Week* Top Fifty recorded combined income of £100,635,448 in 1986 and in 1996 this had risen to £256,879,628. In Germany no directly comparable figures are available but the 35 leading members of the German Public Relations Association which disclose figures, reported 1996 fees of 192 million German marks (US$113 million), in my view, an even faster growth rate.

The numbers reflect the performance of an industry growing at well above the average rate. By another measure, college courses in public relations available in the USA number 150. This surely can only be reflective of a profession that is attractive from several points of view to aspiring youth.

There are some grounds, however, for public relations practitioners of a certain age and from certain countries to have feelings of lack of fulfillment. In spite of the fast growth of public relations worldwide, it is true that many barriers do exist to its growth. This is especially true in countries outside the USA and UK, where public relations is more deeply entrenched and practiced than in many other countries. There are a number of hurdles to be overcome in those nations where the concept of public relations is relatively new, and therefore suspect.

Special problems exist in totalitarian states and linger even when the totalitarian regime is overthrown or abandoned in favor of democracy.

■ Propaganda

One of the insults most abhorred by people in my profession is the use of the term propaganda, suggesting that it is synonymous with public relations. The word is invariably used in discussions when it clearly has a pejorative meaning.

The interchangeability of the terms propaganda and public relations was, in fact, a serious barrier to the development of public relations as practiced today.

After World War II, many people in Germany would have nothing to do with public relations. It is one reason why many of the major German concerns were so late to establish professional public relations departments and use consultancies and agencies. They equated public relations-style communications with propaganda; and they had seen or heard what that master of propaganda, Goebbels, had done to twist the truth and bring their country to war. They never wanted that to happen again. Ergo, "we will not engage in public relations activities for our company, it has an evil smell" was a common attitude in German commerce and industry for about three decades after the war had ended. Decision makers had failed to make the distinction between bona fide public relations and propaganda. Discussions and debates on this topic can engage PR people and journalists in arguments that go deep into the night. It is certainly not possible to resolve the question over a single bottle of wine.

Webster's Dictionary defines propaganda as: 1. a congregation of the Roman curia having jurisdiction over missionary territories and related institutions 2. the spreading of ideas, information, or rumor for the purpose of helping or injuring an institution, a cause, or a person 3. ideas, facts, or allegations spread deliberately to further one's cause or to damage an opposing cause; also: a public action having such an effect.

The Concise Oxford Dictionary's definition is: 1. association or organized scheme for propagation of a doctrine or practice; doctrines, information, etc., thus propagated. 2. committee of cardinals in charge of foreign missions.

However, to me the distinction lies less in the meaning of the word propaganda than in the context in which it is practiced. I would like to propose this definition: "Propaganda is a form of persuasive communication that succeeds in states where there are totalitarian governments and cannot exist in a true democracy."

In other words, Goebbels was able to succeed when his voice or messages were the only ones permitted in Germany. No opposing view was allowed. No debate existed. It was perilous to voice any opinion contrary to the approved government view.

A similar situation existed in China under Mao Ze Dong, and in spite of gigantic steps undertaken in economic liberalization, the silencing of dissenting voices in Tianamen Square showed that there had not been a full embracing of democracy. Public relations can be practiced in only a limited way in China today.

The same can be said about the Soviet Union in the time of Stalin, the Iraq of Saddam Hussein and some of the Islamic states ruled by clerics, such as Iran under the ayatollahs.

■ Censorship

The partner of propaganda is censorship. There are today some places which are "semi-propaganda" states. They are superficially democratic but the media is censored or restricted. Singapore is such an example. Censorship ensures that propaganda is the only form of communication and the distribution of several publications such as the *Wall Street Journal* and the *Far Eastern Economic Review* is strictly controlled.

In the USA there is concern at the concentration of media ownership into just a few hands, along with a similar trend in advertising agencies which hold great commercial power. Some fear for the objectivity of news and current affairs programming.

In many countries, the most dangerous form of media control exists – self censorship. Although it is most prevalent in 'semi-propaganda' states as mentioned earlier, it is also found in places thought to be the freest democracies.

In these cases, editors, broadcast producers and publishers consciously or unconsciously print or broadcast material that is benign to the state or, sometimes, commercial interests. In unwritten agreements, the media refrains from publishing material critical of the political or commercial establishment, its people and policies, in return for the right to publish at all. Even in strongly democratic nations there is a rush to self-censorship, with propaganda flourishing when a major crisis such as total war occurs. An example was Britain in World War II, when an unashamedly-called "government propaganda film industry" was established. Some of its products are still to be seen as re-runs on television. In the climate of those wartime years, any dissenting or opposing views were silenced.

For the international public relations executive, this means the need to be especially sensitive as to what can be achieved through the media and what messages must be conveyed to influencers by other means.

The galvanizing effect on the media when democracy replaces a totalitarian regime is amazing to witness.

An early European example was seen in Spain, where there was the restoration of a constitutional monarchy following the death of the dictator General Franco, in 1969. Even under Franco, Spain had a small cadre of public relations professionals who operated successfully but within the constraints of that strict regime. One of these practitioners, with whom I have had the privilege of working over many years, is Ramon Alvarez. He describes the change of government thus: "Overnight, newsstands appeared on the streets, each full of newspapers and magazines. Some of these had been published underground in previous years but others were completely new. The media in Spain took on a completely new lease on life and topics that had been taboo were now openly discussed in print. TV and radio, which continued to be government controlled, opened up more gradually in the years that followed."

The importance of the flourishing media in Spain was soon to be seen, as reactionaries in Spain who could not get used to the new ways of democracy sought to bring back the fascist regime via a coup which had its climax in the House of Parliament. The coup failed and many believe that it was because Spaniards had had a taste of the new media – and because they were informed of events hour by hour.

The experience of Spain was repeated in Germany, when the Berlin Wall came down, and there was a domino effect throughout Eastern Europe, culminating in the overthrow of communism in Russia itself. In the Americas, recent political developments have led to the creation of a media that is much less pliable in the hands of the ruling party. Mexico is a good example.

In the case of Eastern Europe, the media was an important cause for the rejection of communism, as well as the beneficiary when democracy arrived.

The ability of people at all levels in society to receive TV signals and radio programs from neighboring – and far-off – democracies diminished the power of propaganda's single message.

In this age of channel surfing, how could pontificating party officials compete with quiz shows and soap operas newly available via satellite?

■ Overconfident self-reliance

The quotation from Ralph Waldo Emerson, "Make a better mousetrap and the world will beat a path to your door," is perhaps the biggest lie in the annals of marketing. Similarly, "If you employ a public relations professional, everyone will think you are in trouble or have something to hide" is a most common myth in public relations and one that has actually deterred executives from gaining valuable advice and assistance that might have helped them avoid trouble.

In many countries, it is seen as sufficient to manage business in an efficient way and for the corporation to behave decently. Everything will then take care of itself and the company's reputation will stand high. In fact, some executives and journalists believe this so strongly that they accuse companies that do employ aggressive communications policies of being unduly self-promotional.

This barrier is very easy to understand, especially if you come from a culture that is reserved and repelled by people who are driven by a need for personal recognition and publicity.

Moreover, there is a technical reason which the media finds disturbing. If from time immemorial, senior journalists have dealt directly with the chief executive of the company, they do not usually take kindly to the insertion of an intermediary – a public relations professional – in the relationship, even though it might be to the advantage of both sides.

The media invariably views such an appointment as the erection of a wall between themselves and the company. It is regrettable that too few PR executives who take company positions have the personality and seniority to convince the media that they should be seen as a bridge, not a hurdle, in the relationship.

This is why such appointments should be made during a period of calm in a company's history and not at a time of crisis, lest the myth mentioned earlier come to be reality.

■ Measurability

The difficulties of measuring the effectiveness of public relations have been a serious barrier to its growth over the years. The many-sided nature of public relations and its special branches, prevent measuring in a uniform manner. Different methods to evaluate whether the PR efforts have succeeded or failed are needed for marketing support, public affairs, corporate reputation, employee communications, and philanthropy. Even when the right method of evaluation is known, it is often not used for reasons of cost. Far too often, the cost of research studies to establish the success or failure of a program is greater than the cost of the program itself, and is therefore not undertaken.

In direct response advertising, success and failure are clear to see in the sales that are generated. In public relations, cause-related programs offer the potential of measurement through the speed with which funds are collected and the amount that is eventually amassed for the nominated cause. Similarly, in the arena of public affairs, success or failure is often recorded for all to know at the ballot box.

People in advertising have, over the years, done a much better job of convincing their employers or clients that the effect of advertising can be measured, and indeed, in some cases, just as with PR, there is a clearly measurable result.

In order to justify their huge budgets, advertising agents have developed sophisticated testing and measurement procedures and usually appear in joint meetings with public relations colleagues to have a greater mastery over the techniques of measurement. In truth, they are no more advanced than people in public relations.

The International Committee of Public Relations Consultancies Associations (ICO) has just published a pamphlet on goal setting and measurement. Peter Hehir, Chairman of Countrywide Porter Novelli, whose brainchild it is says: "I hope this guide provides clients and their agencies with a useful guide that will help them to establish realistic objectives."

■ "Soft" image

Public relations' image as a "soft" discipline, lacking in intellectual underpinning and research-based evaluation systems, is probably the most persistent barrier to its development. It is in this area that practitioners of the future should be devoting their greatest attention. The profession might then grow at an even more accelerated pace than in the recent past when, in spite of this and other barriers, the growth of the leading public relations agencies/consultancies has been much greater than that of the top advertising agencies.

■ Low esteem

A longtime hurdle for public relations was the relatively low esteem in which PR practitioners were held, but that is changing for the better, surely one reason the growth of PR has been so strong in recent years.

The profession is clearly very attractive to young people. Fast-increasing public relations undergraduate and master's courses around the world are oversubscribed. Yet, parents would probably have preferred their children to have chosen one of the established older professions such as the law, medicine or architecture. Nevertheless, the difference in the perceived status of public relations and more traditional careers is diminishing. The shift is not, unhappily, just because of the increased standing of public relations as a serious discipline, but because the "god-like" status and respect once accorded to doctors and lawyers has been fast dropping in recent years, as those professions slide from being vocational to commercial.

■ Strength in variety

The variety of public relations specialties and the ability of people from other professions to transfer to this field have given it great strength in today's society. I have known lawyers who have felt imprisoned in law firms, doing routine tasks, envious of us in public relations. While they have been trapped undertaking lengthy and boring interpretations of existing law or drawing up the papers for various transactions, they have observed that public relations people are often involved in the challenging and exciting business of helping to *change* existing law. There are now a number of lawyers practicing public relations and finding that their legal training is of great value.

The same is true of medicine. There are a number of doctors who feel they can achieve more for the health of a wider group of sick people by practicing their profession in the context of mass communications and have switched career to public relations counseling.

■ The troubling transfer

The notion that "anyone can do PR, because it is so easy" has caused many organizations to make a false start in public relations. This has slowed the acceptance of public relations as an important business discipline within countless companies and in the business community at large.

A typical story of a company recognizing that PR can be a useful business tool – and the all-too-common outcome – goes like this:

The CEO arrives one day and informs his management committee that; as part of improving management and market competitiveness, "we are going to go in for this PR thing I read about in *Fortune*/heard about from Joe at the golf club/that is being used by our main rival and is forcing down our market share/heard about at a conference I've just attended."

You can be sure the CEO did not learn about PR from an MBA course he took at one of the elite colleges.

Although PR now attracts many students to its specialist programs, it barely features in the curricula of the majority of MBA courses, according to "The Importance of Public Relations in Graduate Business Programs," a study I conducted for my company[*] in 1993. The initial finding of the study was depressing. Public relations came last in the rating of the most important elements for the career education of marketing professionals. Professor Miland M. Lele of the University of Chicago could not have made things clearer, saying: "I'll be frank, public relations isn't included in our curriculum."

However, there is also a promising situation: half of those who teach marketing say that coverage of public relations now is too light in their curricula; at the same time, more than one quarter believe it will increase in importance in the next five years.

[*] The Importance of Public Relations in Graduate Business Programs, a survey conducted by Edelman Public Relations Worldwide in 1993.

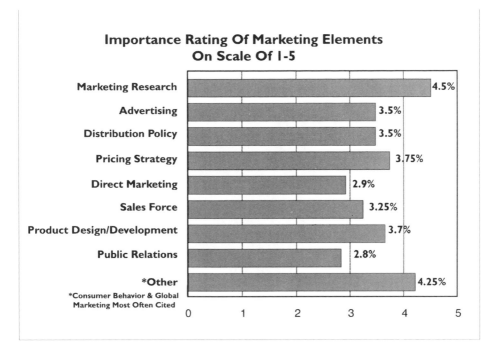

Importance Rating Of Marketing Elements On Scale Of 1-5

- Marketing Research — 4.5%
- Advertising — 3.5%
- Distribution Policy — 3.5%
- Pricing Strategy — 3.75%
- Direct Marketing — 2.9%
- Sales Force — 3.25%
- Product Design/Development — 3.7%
- Public Relations — 2.8%
- *Other — 4.25%

*Consumer Behavior & Global Marketing Most Often Cited

Chart 6.1

■ Methods of improving public relations study

Responding professors offer a wide variety of ways they think understanding of public relations can be improved. Case studies are by far the most frequently mentioned (38.4 per cent) followed by textbooks (16.4 per cent). Guest speakers, computer simulations and outside reading are also mentioned (see chart 6.2).

Case studies are already used in courses in almost half the schools (46.3 per cent).

"I think the only opportunity in my department (marketing) is to develop teaching materials – probably case histories – that raise public relations management issues. I think faculty members would react very appreciatively to new, exciting, dramatic cases," said Peter L. Wright of Stanford University.

"To improve the understanding of public relations among MBA students, state-of-the-art case histories should be developed and used," Paul W. Farris, University of Virginia, agreed.

■ Important aspects of public relations

Within public relations, educators ranked crisis and issues management as the most important aspect of public relations for their students to understand and apply. Media relations ranked second, followed by corporate image and employee communications. Marketing was ranked fifth, followed by government relations and investor relations.

**Ways to Improve
Understanding of Public Relations**

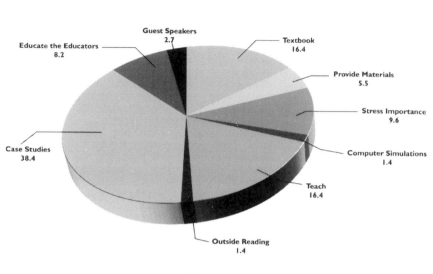

Chart 6.2

Eight in ten survey participants said that less than 20 per cent of the required courses in their MBA programs are devoted to marketing. About the same number (81.3 per cent) said it would be difficult to add a new required course to their curriculum, although most said it would be relatively easy to add an elective course.

Having made the decision to engage in PR activities, a typical company usually assigns the function to a member of its existing staff who is personable, "gets on well with people" and is reasonably persuasive in conversation and on the written page. Sadly, his likely most striking credential is his availability, because he is no longer as effective as he once was in his current position (perhaps a sales manager). The company has no wish to dismiss him but is watching out for opportunities to transfer him to other duties. The PR position sounds perfect!

Such transferees sometimes make a decent go of the job and prepare the way for the appointment of professional, trained staff, in due course. Others, I fear, put back the cause by several years, through no fault of their own.

The problem, which would be immensely helped by the introduction of some PR modules in the MBA courses, arises because there is little understanding of the art and science of persuasive communication, its strategic purpose or the technology of message delivery, all of which are essential to the effective use of PR.

It is no longer true that "anybody can do it", if ever it was.

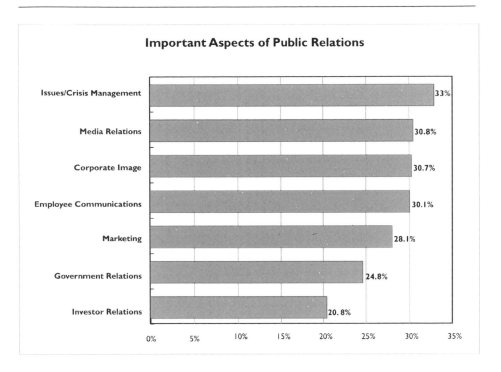

Important Aspects of Public Relations

Issues/Crisis Management	33%
Media Relations	30.8%
Corporate Image	30.7%
Employee Communications	30.1%
Marketing	28.1%
Government Relations	24.8%
Investor Relations	20.8%

Chart 6.3

■ The hidden persuaders

Vance Packard's book, *The Hidden Persuaders*, published in 1957, had an important impact on the development of the entire field of persuasive communication, including public relations. The book turned out to be both a barrier and a force for growth of the field.

On the one hand, many people (well beyond the number of those who had actually read the book) were repelled by the sinister suggestion that people could easily be manipulated by various communications techniques, including subliminal messages. They wanted to have nothing to do with it.

Others recognized that understanding and using these techniques were the path to power and success in business or politics.

Before Packard's thesis, there had always been public concern about the potential for sinister manipulation of people – individuals and groups. The concern will continue as long as the earth turns. The public has a huge appetite for stories of possibly evil manipulators, such as the *eminence grise*, Cardinal Richelieu and the boy king, Rasputin and the Tsar and Tsarina, and Svengali and Trilby.

More recently there has been much public debate in the USA about the power of unelected political strategists and communicators who are no longer the hidden persuaders made famous by Vance Packard. Now they are themselves celebrities, whose views are discussed in the political columns and whose private lives feed the gossip columns of the media.

Their importance has increased, as has the complexity and balance of modern politics, along with the need to understand the way in which the media must be used for electoral success. Political leadership relies as much on expediency – polling to chart a course most acceptable to public opinion – as it does on deeply held convictions. There is great concern that unelected advisers exercise too great an influence on policy decisions.

The whole topic was summed up in a remark made by Larry Speakes, White House spokesman in the Reagan Administration, who claimed that "When the President opens his mouth, it is my words that come out."

■ An American art

The American-developed art of electoral campaign strategy, surely a subset of the broad field of public relations, has been exported to politicians in many countries by pioneering counseling firms in this field, such as Sawyer Miller Associates. And, while some see this as an unfortunate development, who can argue with the fact that it goes hand in hand with the growth of democracy? The need for such advice only exists where there is debate among political opponents, with resolution taking place at the ballot box. The clients of these firms (among them the Philippines, Colombia, Panama, Peru, Brazil, Turkey) are often ones that have sought to find their way in democracy after years under totalitarian systems of one sort or another, as well as very long-established democracies such as Britain, where the Prime Minister and leader of the Labour Party, Tony Blair, sought the strategic advice of George Stephanopoulos, a former chief spokesman for President Clinton.

None of the formidable barriers mentioned in this chapter have impeded the steady progress of public relations during the second half of the twentieth century. They have been dismantled by an increasingly well-educated world public with a thirst for information and material products. That thirst is being slaked by global media empires and producers of goods and services that use the proliferating new channels of communication.

Even the fear of propaganda and manipulation by hidden or famous persuaders has been countered by the recognition of the power of skilled communications to affect the hearts and minds of people and their voting or purchasing decisions. As the power of the professional communicator's skills is increasingly recognized, so more recruits are added, prestige is increased, new tools of measurement are being found. No longer does PR stand for "poor relation" among the professions.

CHAPTER 7

The Specialization of International Public Relations

Specialization, globalization and communications technology are currently the three most potent forces affecting the practice of international public relations.

Of these, specialization has had the longest history and the greatest impact over the past three decades.

Until the mid-1960s, public relations was a calling for generalists, whether they worked in-house at companies or in consultancies or agencies. As a youthful profession or craft, it also had to draw its recruits from other fields, mostly journalism, which at that time was also much more general than it is today. The business, arts, travel and other specialists sections in the newspapers of today are a relatively new invention. Journalists and PR people were expected to put their hand – and brain – to any task that came along.

The public relations officers (as they were mostly called) in most companies were expected to offer product publicity support on Monday, conduct interviews, write and lay out the employee newsletter on Tuesday, arrange a community sponsorship activity on Wednesday, write the Chairman's statement for the annual report on Thursday and be ready on Friday to diffuse a crisis with consummate skill. (Crises always occur on Fridays, usually at about 5:00 p.m.) Over the weekend, he would be expected to study complicated reports from a management consultant, recommending a divisional reorganization. He needed to be ready on Monday with a plan to make the announcements internally and externally, and to prepare the executives involved with the presentation of their speeches. He would be expected to hone the key messages and to conduct media training.

The public relations executive at the consultancy or agency, meanwhile, would have to be able to take exactly the same week as his in-house opposite number in his stride. But he would also have to be knowledgeable and flexible enough to undertake the same functions for a variety of client organizations, ranging from pharmaceutical companies through producers of consumer products to banks and financial institutions or government departments.

It was clear this could not last. The huge horizon of public relations activity, which defies easy definition, demanded that it be broken down into manageable components. And in the intervening years this has happened with a vengeance.

From a situation in which almost every practitioner had started life in a job outside public relations, we have moved to a point where not only have some spent their entire working life in public relations, but some in their thirties and forties have spent it in a single specialty, often without even the opportunity to glimpse the wider world of their profession.

This is one of the conundrums facing public relations today. Many feel that the pressure of specialization detracts from the true contribution that public relations can make at the corporate level. Specialization results in too little broad perspective, too little general knowledge, too little awareness of the full range of shapes and dynamics that make up our societies.

And in the concerns about the narrow view of the universe that accompanies intense specialization, include a worry that too little attention is paid to international affairs.

I have to admit that one of the attractions of public relations to me when I started out was the opportunity to be involved in a huge range of industries and activities, and to draw on as many skills as I could possibly attain. No two days needed to be the same. The lessons of one project or assignment invariably found a useful application in another, and perhaps in a different industry. After 37 years in practice, it is this variety that still keeps me interested, challenged and learning.

On the other hand, the magnet of specialization is too strong to resist.

■ Why specialization?

Four factors are at work. The first is the increased recognition of the importance of public relations by different industries. This has meant the allocation of increasingly large budgets which, in turn, call for greater numbers of dedicated, qualified personnel.

The second factor is the accelerating complexity of almost every industry, as the knowledge base of science-driven fields of endeavor increases exponentially each year. The data that has to be mastered by anyone professing to be a communicator in any sector is enormous. Few are gifted enough to be truly able to work at the most detailed level in more than one industry. This factor has also made the practice of public relations itself, on behalf of any industry, more challenging in terms of the techniques and technology used.

The third factor is an increasingly educated and inquisitive consumer public served by a newly aggressive and growing media, which is itself structured on specialist lines.

The fourth force driving specialization has been the emergence of many industries and professions which traditionally had shunned communications. In some cases, as with law and medicine, self-imposed or common-law regulations forbade self promotion. Many of those taboos have been torn down.

A careful look at the PR league tables shows that the engines of growth in recent years have been the boutique agencies which have offered specialist PR services of some kind. Even the major international full-service agencies mostly owe their successful growth to the performance of their individual specialist divisions.

■ Categories of specialization

What are these specialties, and how have they reshaped the public relations landscape?

There are three kinds:

- *Industry, business or organization.* There are discrete PR specialties in Healthcare and Pharmaceutical Products, Consumer Products and Services, Financial Service Organizations, Technology, Defense, Professional Services and many more.
- *PR practice areas.* No matter what industry, there are PR specialties in Investor Relations, Public Affairs, Community Relations, Employee Communications, Sponsorship and Event Management.
- *Technical skills.* Within PR structures, there are specialist roles played by dedicated experts in publications, speechwriting, video production, media relations, CDrom and Website development, and a number of other functions.

Just when you think you have grasped the full meaning of specialization, it becomes apparent that this is a continuous process of sub-division. Nowadays, even the specialties within specialties can support relatively large PR practices. An example can be found in the broad specialty of technology. There are individual PR practitioners who spend their entire working week narrowly focused on semi-conductors or systems software, of which they have to have extensive knowledge. These same people may not be able to work effectively in other branches of technology.

The movement toward specialization began in the mid-1960s with pharmaceuticals and with the investor relations branch of financial public relations, two of the three specialties that are still the most dynamic within PR. The third major specialty, technology, began its dramatic growth two decades later.

These three specialties are also the most "portable" and international in the whole field of public relations, and so are of great interest and importance to the international practitioner.

I have not included one of the largest specialties – consumer products and services – because it constituted a major sector even in the earliest days of PR. It continues to be hugely important within PR as a whole, but having started on a high plateau it has not demonstrated the exceptional growth of the other three specialties. It has, however, changed in the demands that it makes on practitioners, and this is discussed later in this chapter.

■ Pharmaceuticals

The description "ethical" for pharmaceuticals that were available to the public only with a doctor's prescription gives a hint about how the medical profession, producers and pharmacists viewed the broad industry group to which their fortunes were so closely tied. A stronger clue was the terminology usually applied to what are now known as over-the-counter drugs (OTCs), which were described either as "patent" or "proprietary" medicines.

In the first 50 years of the century, not only did doctors, as the sole source of prescriptions, control the sales of ethical drugs, they also controlled all information about these preparations. There was limited public awareness of available treatments. Physicians were apt to be testy when confronted by knowledgeable patients who might wish to discuss alternative forms of treatment. This was particularly true in the majority of countries where healthcare was socialized and the major "buyers" of prescription pharmaceuticals were governments.

The manufacturers of ethical pharmaceuticals were the self-same companies that made medicines that were sold over the counter with advertising and public relations support. They could see the power of communications to inform, educate and persuade the public in health-related matters.

No one ever dreamed that the day would arrive when prescription-only drugs would be advertised to the public in general print and TV media, as has been the case since the early 1990s in the USA (albeit under tight control). Pharmaceutical companies turned in increasing numbers to public relations practitioners to step in and fill the informational and promotional gap.

We were entering an era of discovery of new life-saving or life-improving compounds for millions of sufferers, and even the birth of new sciences and production methods such as biotechnology. Pharmaceutical manufacturers wanted to tell the world. There were time and competitive pressures as well. The companies knew they had to make and grow their markets in time to achieve an adequate return on the investment in R&D during the 14-year life of their patents. If another manufacturer was on the same trail, it was important to establish a strong and secure market position which would be hard for the new rival to penetrate. The manufacturers could no longer leave this entirely in the hands of the medical profession, which was thought to move at a glacial pace.

Initial assignments were well within the scope of generalist PR practitioners. Then, the demands of parallel-track communications, both to and through the medical and pharmacy professions, as well as to the end user via the general media, called for more specialist PR knowledge. As the PR specialty developed, it attracted doctors, pharmacologists, pharmacists, chemists and other communicators with a special interest in and aptitude for these subjects. It has continued that way ever since and is now one of the two largest specialist sectors of public relations. The other is technology.

It has created its own sub-specialties which correspond directly with various medical specialties, such as cardiology, nephrology, oncology and sports medicine; health economics and politics; hospitals and other care-giving institutions; health professional groups; home delivery of health care; sub-divisions by gender, race, age; science writing; biotechnology; ethics; continuing medical education; meetings organization, and patient groups.

Pharmaceutical companies have also fueled the internationalization of public relations. Most of the leading companies have been active internationally for several decades and, almost without exception, their major products have worldwide application.

Although it is still exceptional for any new drug to be launched in all markets simultaneously, the data need to support approval to market is increasingly accepted among most advanced countries. Thus the roll out of a new preparation now usually takes place over a relatively short period. It is customary for pharmaceutical companies to develop the blueprint of a pre-marketing program, launch the campaign centrally, and then adapt and implement it locally in all key markets.

The movement toward specialization which is now deeply rooted in the USA and the UK is less pronounced in the smaller or newer markets for public relations. In many of these, the size of the business, the scarcity of qualified PR people and the continuing strict application of rules governing communications related to prescription drugs all work against the development of specialized PR practices on a comparable scale.

The size of the specialist market for healthcare public relations is evident in the growing annual figures recorded by *O'Dwyer's Directory of PR firms*. The most recent table of top ten firms (for the year 1996) is shown below.

HEALTHCARE

1. Burson-Marsteller	$60,656,923
2. Porter Novelli International	24,132,000
3. Edelman PR Worldwide	23,621,806
4. Shandwick	18,601,000
5. Ruder Finn	17,020,000
6. Ogilvy Adams & Rinehart	16,400,000
7. Ketchum Public Relations	16,100,000
8. Manning, Selvage & Lee	13,504,000
9. Fleishman-Hillard	11,204,000
10. GCI Group	9,475,481

Chart 7.1

■ Financial

The growth of financial public relations has been powered by a battery of forces combining to create a major practice area.

Increasing individual wealth in many countries has multiplied the number of individual share owners. Unit trusts and mutual funds have attracted huge sums of money from investors, allowing them the chance to participate in baskets of stocks of every kind. The media coverage of the performance of companies makes heroes (or villains) out of those who lead them and has captivated large audiences previously unmoved by the making of money or the movements of markets.

Internationalization of money markets and the world's major stock exchanges and the introduction of 24-hour trading in stock shares and bonds have supercharged the growth of international financial communications.

As if this were not enough, the fall of communism created millions of potential new capitalists. With the retreat of socialism came the worldwide fashion of privatization of utilities and other government or nationalized industries and services, an investment bonanza that made shareholders out of entire new population segments in many countries.

Increased wealth and wider share ownership demanded explosive growth in the financial services industry. Millions of people whose previous contact with financial matters had been through a bank account and one or two insurance policies were no longer content to leave their future prosperity in the hands of the old-fashioned bank manager. More and more took an interest in their savings, investments, and insurance policies. They came into the market for home ownership. Credit and debit cards entered their lives.

Banks, payments services companies, insurance companies, brokerage houses and other financial institutions became major employers of PR executives and PR agencies.

The popularization of share ownership and use of the instruments marketed by financial services companies occurred at the same time as another phenomenon, which acted as a turbocharger to the growth of financial public relations practice – a tidal wave of mergers and acquisitions, through which huge industrial consolidations have taken place. Many of these were hotly contested, which meant that fulsome fees were generated by the PR firms that had established a sub-specialty in "M&A" (mergers and acquisitions) communications and were battle-ready to assist the predator or defending company.

When the current fashion of "divestiture" arrived as a counterpoint to the continuing merger mania, PR practitioners needed to explain the logic behind the decision to split a company into two or more parts. And then they had to convince investors of the potential value of the shares of each part. This has merely added another sub-specialty to the list of PR skills, and a new source of income besides.

The important position held by financial public relations within the universe of public relations practice is shown in the O'Dwyer fee rankings for financial public relations firms.

Although both require a mastery of finance, public relations on behalf of financial institutions that sell products and services (insurance policies, mutual funds, mortgages, etc.) and investor relations are two quite different practices.

Internationally, investor relations (IR) as a general rule does not even report through the public relations channel to top management. Most public companies have vice presidents (or directors) of investor relations whose direct reporting line is to the chief financial officer, who in turn reports to the CEO. In only a few companies does the senior IR executive report to a chief communications officer.

IR in the USA even has its own professional organization, the National Institute of Investor Relations (NIRI). Similar organizations exist in other countries, operating outside the orbit of public relations organizations.

Like most other PR practitioners, beyond working with the media, IR specialists are heavily engaged in routine activities. Many of these are optional and just make good sense. Others are required by law or by rules of the regulating authorities. The USA, which probably requires the most disclosure of any country, is regulated by the Securities and Exchange Commission (SEC), which dictates what must be disclosed and when; it also investigates violations and imposes penalties on those who transgress. For instance, the SEC requires institutions that have $100 million or more in assets under management to file quarterly reports of their holdings. These filings are compiled and issued as public record, and are accessible through many databases.

IR practitioners can thank the tide of increasing regulation for expanding their career opportunities. When new disclosure requirements hit companies unfamiliar with the techniques of communicating information, this led to the creation of a major new area of PR practice.

Among the routine tasks undertaken by the head of investor relations are:

- production of the annual report. The most important document produced by any public company, this document must act as a brochure, resource guide and promotional vehicle with a life of 12 months. Always in printed form, the reports of many companies now also have website and video versions;
- preparation of periodic interim reports, quarterly in the USA, semi-annually in many other countries, declaring financial results;
- a conference call to the analysts who follow the company's shares and to the media, within hours of the issue of financial results. Almost obligatory, this procedure allows the company to elaborate on the factors that contributed to the results and share expectations for the future;
- writing speeches the CEO and CFO will deliver to financial audiences and arranging one-to-one interviews with key journalists;
- organizing road shows, traveling presentations undertaken once a year or every two years. A team of senior company officers visits key cities in the home country in which there are important financial institutions or shareholders; less frequently, they take the show to foreign financial capitals. The events are orchestrated to reassure current stockholders and to attract new buyers.

For the IR specialist, there are two targets – the shareholder and those who might influence shareholder decisions. The problem is that many shareholders want to remain anonymous and their holdings are in the names of nominee accounts.

It is useful to know exactly who these people are in tranquil times. But it becomes vitally important in a contested acquisition, merger or other dispute.

Finding out the entire shareholder base is complicated and involves purchasing data from the specialist organizations known as proxy solicitors. They provide the names of all shareholders directly to the company in advance of the annual shareholder meeting. These firms send out, collect and tabulate the proxy votes for the meeting. Two leading proxy solicitation companies are D.F. King & Co. Inc. and Morrow & Co. Inc.

National depository companies where certificates are exchanged, such as Philadelphia Depository Trust Co. (Philadep) and The Depository Trust Company (DTC), are also repositories for stocks, bonds and other securities. Transfer agents, primarily commercial banks, keep the records and issue and destroy certificates.

In addition to these types of service firms, there are businesses that specialize in identifying and analyzing shareholders on a real-time basis. They utilize proprietary databases and sophisticated screening techniques to monitor changes in shareholder composition. This service is particularly important, for example, when a company needs to determine who is behind increased volume in share trading or unusual price movement. Among the leading firms that offer shareholder identification on a global basis are Corporate Investor Communications, Inc., Carson Group, Technimetrics, D.F. King & Co., Inc., and First Chicago Trust Company.

Some of the largest IR/Financial PR firms are not included in the list that follows because they do not reveal their income. The total is impressive. Possibly the largest in the specialty is Kekst & Company, in the USA.

FINANCIAL PR/INVESTOR RELATIONS	
1. Burson-Marsteller	$48,845,282
2. Fleishman-Hillard	42,400,000
3. Shandwick	26,575,000
4. Edelman PR Worldwide	24,382,290
5. Financial Relations Board	20,224,882
6. Morgen-Walke	16,504,000
7. Porter Novelli International	13,958,000
8. Ogilvy Adams & Rinehart	13,300,000
9. GCI Group	9,242,832
10. Bozell Sawyer Miller Group	9,200,000

© Copyright 1997 The J.R. O'Dwyer Co. Inc.

Chart 7.2

■ Technology

Anyone practicing public relations in the financial sector today will testify to the importance of technology as possibly the single most critical element in the economies of the developed world.

Technology stocks have, for some investors, even taken over as the barometer of performance of the stock market from the traditional baskets of blue chip shares such as the FTSE in the UK, The Dow Jones Index and the Hang Seng in Hong Kong.

For example, rumors early in 1997 that the long-running bull market would come to an end were based on the expectation that the sizzling demand for personal computers and their ancillary products had slowed down.

When category leader Microsoft produced results that were double the expectations of all experts, it was the trigger that enabled the entire US stock market to record one of its largest-ever daily increases.

This leadership among investments was the result of technology's explosive growth over three decades, with the arrival of Clive Sinclair in Britain and Steve Jobs, Paul Allen and Bill Gates in the USA.

At the heart of this phenomenon was the personal computer, which put at the fingertips of millions of individuals the information processing and communications capability that just a few years earlier had been available only to major corporations. Along with government departments, only they had the ability to invest in large mainframe machines housed in air-conditioned temples and tended by high priests who were the only people familiar with the binary codes needed to converse with the gods of calculus.

Bill "Microsoft" Gates' dream of a computer in every home is well on its way to becoming reality. And many of those terminals are connected to each other directly or through that phenomenon of the 1990s, the Internet.

Technology advances arrived on cue, year after year. As machines became smaller as well as less expensive, they grew in power and range of functions.

All the while, other, related technologies blossomed to serve and augment the personal computer. In every phase of industry and the professions, in government, in retailing and banking, computing power combined with connectivity and the ability to store massive amounts of data.

Today's personal computers can design, control production and inventories, record, accept orders, buy raw materials, control deliveries and sales, audit performance, and undertake many other functions.

If money represents the building blocks of the new global economy, technology is the cement that will hold them together. These are the two most international specialties within the entire field of public relations. And according to the statistics collected by O'Dwyer, in 1996 Technology overtook Healthcare to become the largest specialty within public relations.

Just like financial PR, technology communications is now made up of a mosaic of sub-specialties. The boutique agencies that were established less than a decade ago, along with specialist technology units at the major full-service agencies, have blossomed into powerhouses in their own right. They have divided into units dedicated to a large range of clients in sub-sectors of the information technology industry – among them, semi-conductors and microprocessors, business and personal software, internet access, website development, PCs, servers, mainframes, supercomputers, telephony and wireless.

The pitch of complexity of each of these areas is such to demand the full attention of highly qualified specialist teams of executives. Admittedly, a truly skilled PR executive should have the knack of communicating quite arcane concepts to the average, intelligent lay audience well enough to impart a good general understanding of the subject. But he first needs to be able to understand and communicate in the jargon and shorthand used by his peers in the industry – and the specialist media that serves it. At that level, the discussions will appear to be in an obscure foreign language to most members of the general public.

The O'Dwyer ranking of the leading firms practicing technology communications is shown in chart 7.3.

The three cornerstones of internationalization and specialization of public relations – Healthcare, Financial and Technology – are followed by several other specialties based on industry, business or type of organization.

HIGH-TECH	
1. Shandwick	$47,663,000
2. Porter Novelli International including Brodeur Porter Novelli and Copithorne & Bellows	37,449,000
3. Burson-Marsteller	37,143,756
4. Edelman PR Worldwide	26,843,033
5. Cunningham Communication	15,661,623
6. Fleishman-Hillard	15,550,000
7. The Weber Group	14,595,193
8. Manning, Selvage & Lee	12,889,000
9. GCI Group	11,043,005
10. Technology Solutions	10,795,000

Chart 7.3

■ Consumer products and services

Do not be fooled into thinking that this specialty does not require a great deal of expertise and detailed knowledge. Today's consumers are better educated and more selective than ever. They have been bombarded with information about their consumer rights. Many say their purchasing decisions are affected by factors beyond the price, appearance and performance of a product or service.

For example, in food PR, it is not sufficient to promote a product using an appealing photograph and offering a recipe that works. Now editors and their readers will want details about the nutritional value of the item, its fat and calorie content. The PR practitioner also needs to know if any of the ingredients has been under suspicion as being a carcinogen.

The consumer will want to know about the safety of toys, the side effects of over-the-counter medications, the chemicals used in gardening products, whether cosmetics have been tested on animals (such as the Draze test for eye make-up), or if packaging is recyclable.

In the broad consumer field there are PR specialties in: Food and Nutrition, Household Durables, Fashion and Beauty, Luxury Goods, the Home Office, Entertainment and the Arts, Personal Finance. Because of the size of the industries they encompass, some consumer sub-specialties deserve special mention.

Automobiles: Cars have been the driving force in many economies for so long that automobile PR has taken root as a well-defined specialty. It has for many years also been practiced both locally and internationally. Ford is in the vanguard of top companies with a truly global strategy. Automobile PR offers career scope for practitioners with similar aspirations. Anyone hoping to reach the senior-most position in an automobile-manufacturing company will have mastered the PR specialties of consumer product marketing, dealer communications, event planning and organization, and sponsorship and sports marketing. (Almost every car company is heavily involved in motor sport, as a marketing activity.)

Travel & Tourism and Hospitality: This is often considered a full-fledged specialty in its own right but I consider it to be a sub-specialty in consumer communications. It supports the employment of a huge number of PR practitioners and by definition it is international, calling for special skills in multi-country operations. At the heart of international T&T public relations lies "destination marketing", the campaigns undertaken by the governmental national tourist boards of the countries (or cities or resorts) for which tourism is a major foreign currency earner.

These budgets, many of which are eagerly sought by T&T specialist agencies, are large by industry standards. They are usually augmented by the process known as "matching funds", in which the government tourist authority will add one dollar to every dollar spent on approved activities by hotel and resort owners or state and city authorities. Other discrete branches of T&T PR involve work for Hotels; Restaurants; Carriers (airlines, railways, car rental, etc.); Cruise Lines; Theme Parks; Tour Operators and Travel Agencies: Payments Systems (Traveler's Checks, Credit Cards); and Computer Reservation Systems. More recently, a clearly defined practice area concentrating on the business traveler has emerged, as Airlines, Hotels, Car Rental Companies and Credit Card issuers have seen that it is the business traveler in a suit and not the tourist in shorts who delivers the most profit.

Consumer Technology: A recent development, this practice covers products based on increasingly sophisticated technology, and not confined to the home computer. It touches on every gadget in common use – cooking equipment, the telephone and home fax, the photographic camera and the entertainment center.

■ Government

Although there is now increased mobility between the public and private sectors in many countries, there are PR practitioners who choose to spend a lifetime's career in government service. This can be an attractive option for people wanting to practice internationally, if they can get a post in the foreign service or the ministry responsible for tourism. The former usually ensures intervals of postings as press attaché or counselor in embassies abroad. Legions of practitioners also work at the state, county or local governmental level, either as career civil servants or, in countries where that is the custom, as political appointees. Branches of government (such as the military, police forces and postal services) continue to employ large staffs engaged in communications.

■ Defense

There is a relatively small but highly skilled segment of PR practitioners who work in the defense sector, mostly for companies that manufacture aircraft, missiles, tanks, radar systems and similar products, whose only customers are governments.

■ Economic development and trade relations

A cursory look at *The Economist, Business Week, Industries Week* and similar publications will ensure the eye spots several attractive, full- or double-page ad spreads extolling the benefits of investing in a particular country or state or development region. Such advertising has been one of the fastest growing categories in recent years, as emerging nations, developed nations and others undergoing industrial transformations have vied for the infusion of external investment to create jobs and build a modern industrial infrastructure. Educated, skilled labor, space, tax holidays/exemptions, subsidies – all were offered as enticements in an arena that is now extremely competitive.

Budgets for public relations professionals and firms specialized in economic development have been parallel to those for advertising and the work now represents a major practice area in our profession. Many of the techniques used with effect in programs of this type are featured in the case study "Advantage Israel", which won the International Public Relations Association Golden World Award in 1995 and 1996, and a Public Relations Society of America Silver Anvil in 1996.

■ Advantage Israel case history

The Government of Israel Economic Mission (GIEM) develops and expands trade and investment between Israel and the United States. It is the central source for companies seeking not only information on Israel's economic climate but also guidance on doing business with Israel. In 1995, a turbulent year for Israel that ended with the assassination of Prime Minister Yitzhak Rabin, GIEM had to communicate to US corporate decision makers that Israel remained a safe, stable and profitable place in which to do business. The campaign needed to overcome the prejudices of reporters who considered Israel, as one producer for a national business cable network said, "too small to cover". GIEM also had to communicate the growing benefits of investing in Israel and the strategic importance of foreign investment to the peace process.

Working with Edelman Public Relations Worldwide, GIEM introduced itself as a source for the national business and financial press. The Economic Minister and local economic consuls were introduced to regional media. A series of media and business-to-business events was orchestrated throughout the year, to bring GIEM messages to a targeted audience of business, financial and media executives. GIEM mounted a multi-industry trade campaign, which included organizing trade journalist trips to Israel and disseminating information packages.

There was a steady stream of media alerts, story ideas and by-lined articles. A joint speaking engagement was arranged for Israel's Economic Minister to North America and Jordan's Trade Commissioner, which achieved major media coverage. Sensitive to political and economic changes throughout the year, the campaign quickly responded when Yitzhak Rabin was assassinated.

The results included significant and numerous national business and trade media placements with a strong focus on the economy and massive reach through national print, television and radio. Best of all, the Economic Mission registered a 75 per cent increase in inquiries by business and financial leaders and a 25 per cent increase in US business delegations traveling to Israel to seek investment opportunities.

■ Not-for-profit organizations

Many PR practitioners have a vocation to work in non-profit organizations. These can range from long-established charitable organizations such as the International Red Cross (or Crescent) and their national namesakes, or Boys and Girl Scouts, to the newer and more aggressive pressure groups, many of which have a single agenda, for example, Greenpeace in the environmental movement and People for the Ethical Treatment of Animals (PETA), a group seeking the abolition of animal testing. Many of these organizations operate very locally, on a community basis, while others are global in their activities and reach.

■ Professional services

Until recently, any form of promotional activity by the traditional professions was forbidden.

Lawyers, doctors, accountants, architects, pharmacists were strictly regulated by their own associations and tribunals that policed codes of conduct and imposed penalties and sanctions for infractions. Self promotion was forbidden, carefully monitored and severely punished.

How times have changed in the past 20 years.

Now, in many countries, malpractice and divorce lawyers advertise for clients in TV commercials sandwiched between others for automobiles and dishwashing detergent.

Billboards proclaim the wonders achieved by plastic surgeons and penile prosthesis. International accounting firms' logos are seen at sponsored golf tournaments as well as in clever advertising, usually with the message, "we are clever".

Public relations techniques have proven to be a most potent weapon in the professional services marketing armory. Among effective PR tools are straightforward publicity that produces media recognition for work done; case histories of successful client work; and speeches carefully honed for delivery at seminars where every delegate is a potential client.

Professional service organizations have quickly become masters of major creative PR initiatives. For example, Ernst & Young (E&Y) sought to support their goal of "getting in on the ground floor" with clients that have potential to grow big, by creating an "Entrepreneur of the Year" award. The 1996 E&Y Entrepreneur of the Year PR campaign was itself an award winner, taking a Golden World Award in the annual International Public Relations Association contest.

■ Ernst & Young Entrepreneur of the Year case history

Ernst & Young (E&Y), the professional services firm, wanted to reinforce awareness of its ability to help owner-managed, middle-market businesses in the US. With Edelman Public Relations Worldwide, the firm created the Entrepreneur of the Year Awards in 1994, to honor owner-managers of the country's fastest-growing entrepreneurial businesses, with revenues between $2 million and $250 million.

The program consisted of awards in 11 categories, for which contenders could be nominated by their employees, bankers, lawyers, and advertising and public relations advisers. Winners in 46 participating regions would be finalists for national awards, given later in the year during a conference and awards event in New York.

From the start, the program generated national attention. There were 1,000 nominations the first year, whose average annual revenue was $55 million. Business and trade media covered the regional and national winners.

With year-long publicity efforts, E&Y and Edelman were able to capture even better results and entries the following year, but they hit the jackpot in 1996 because they were challenged to come up with fresh ideas for an established program. In addition to persistent publicity efforts all year, they got mileage out of these elements:

- a new, 80-page Entrepreneur of the Year Magazine honoring award recipients and discussing how entrepreneurs shape the US economy, for distribution to prospective clients, elected officials, attendees at the final event and conference, and business and trade media;
- a four-page editorial inset in the Money section of *USA Today*;
- seven full-page advertisements in *USA Today* during the nomination-solicitation period;
- Eleven 30-second video news releases on the national award recipient, sent to 700 television stations;
- a two-hour nationally syndicated radio program taped at the awards event for later broadcast by the WOR Radio network to its 100 stations nationwide;
- two high-profile national sponsors who lent their names to the program – *USA Today* and the Center for Entrepreneurial Leadership of the Ewing Marion Kaufmann Foundation.

As a result, the third year of the program delivered 3,500 nominations; the nominations were of higher quality, with award recipients averaging $125 million in annual revenues; 1,700 entrepreneurs and business leaders attended the culminating event; and the extensive media coverage included Cable News Network (CNN), CNBC, local television stations in major markets, *USA Today*, and regional and trade publications.

■ Trade associations

Many long-established companies gained their first experience with public relations through their membership in an industry organization or trade association. These were the vehicles for many years through which companies would make common cause to build markets for their products, so that they could focus on competitive activity to capture the biggest possible share of expanding markets.

Associations also acted as a single voice through which all members of an industry could represent their united views to government. While some trade associations still do undertake positive, proactive market-building programs, their PR personnel and agencies are generally more heavily engaged in defensive communications programs, issues management and educational efforts.

Today's wisdom among those who direct public relations programs at companies is that good news should be issued by the company but when there is bad news, the company should protect itself behind the defensive shield of the industry trade association. This attitude and policy have reduced the appeal of trade association PR jobs for many practitioners.

A relative of the traditional trade association has emerged as an important new player on the communications scene: the ad hoc coalition, or alliance, formed specifically to promote or fight legislation. If there is a long-term agenda, the life of a coalition may be long, usually it ends its existence on the conclusion of the legislative process.

An example of a multi-country program by an association is the following, conducted in Europe for the Association of Plastics Manufacturers in Europe (APME).

■ Association of Plastics Manufacturers in Europe case history

When the Association of Plastics Manufacturers in Europe (APME) in the mid-1990s identified young people as key influencers of environmental decisions, the association conducted research which indicated several challenges in any efforts to make students aware of the contributions of plastics to society.

1. A pan-European PR program would demand recognition of country-by-country cultural and educational differences.
2. There would be a perception that the APME initiative would 'flood' schools with pro-plastics messages and that would generate opposition.
3. Materials going to schools would have to appeal both to teachers and to students.
4. A previous absence of positive information in schools and a barrage of material from environmental pressure groups had generated a negative image of plastics.

Taking these concerns into account, APME created and implemented an ambitious and strategically driven program with Countrywide Porter Novelli that was more powerful and more readily accepted than anything the association's 40 member companies could have achieved individually.

A timetable was established for pilot education programs in 1994–95 in France, Germany, Italy and the UK, to be extended in 1996–97 to Belgium, Denmark, Finland, the Netherlands, Norway, Spain and Sweden. Teachers were consulted extensively at all stages to develop credible, useful in-school resource packets and activities that would engage students. Panels of industry members and educators shaped program messages. Because curricula differed widely across countries, the packets were tailored to local needs and cultural differences. Student involvement would be generated by an essay contest on the theme, "Plastics Make It Possible", held at country and pan-European levels.

One example of country customization was the program in France, where teachers needed the endorsement of education authorities to engage in the proposed activities. APME and Porter/Novelli worked with school inspectors to distribute the packets directly to teachers and meet with them.

A launch event took place at the Design Museum in London, with European media, key industry representatives and educators attending. A direct-mail letter and response card went to teachers, offering educational packets and contest details which were sent out only when requested. Country-specific media relations programs followed, to encourage contest entries, targeting education, trade and regional/national media. A host of other PR tools were set in motion: by-lined articles, speaker opportunities, radio interviews, newsletters that students helped produce and which were translated into three languages, helplines for teachers, meetings with influential shapers of education and environment policy, and industry-representative visits to schools – all of these also individualized country-by-country.

Sixty students entered the first competition. National winners attended a European final at an international plastics exhibition in Germany, covered by 80 journalists from across Europe, with numerous important plastics customers, industry leaders and Members of the European Parliament attending.

The program, which won the Institute of Public Relations Sword of Excellence award in 1997, resulted in requests for materials from 22,000 teachers, reaching nearly one million students; positive student perceptions of plastics as observed by teachers; extensive coverage in general, education, business and trade media across Europe; support and even additional budgets from APME member companies; recognition as part of the European Union's Year of Lifelong Learning; and presentation at a conference supported by the European Commission's Directorate General for Education, Training and Youth.

■ Business to business

The field of business to business communications is difficult to define because it spans a number of industries and, therefore, is not included in most of the PR rankings of specialist firms; it is the industries themselves that are deemed to be the specialist practice areas.

Nevertheless, communications on behalf of companies for which the end-consumer is another business have special characteristics. For one thing, there is usually nothing equivalent to a consumer supermarket or department store. Very often, buying decisions are not made by a single individual but by a group of people, all of whom have a say in the selection of the purchase.

Some business to business companies are: office equipment; raw materials needed for added value processing; industrial equipment; transport services; employment agencies; and consultancy services.

There are also business to business divisions of companies which sell directly to individual consumers for home use. One example is telephone service. AT&T's Business Services division had sales of $26 billion in 1996 compared with the $24 billion recorded for private customers. Other illustrations are the catering divisions of food producers that predominantly sell to restaurants and hotels; the commercial and industrial divisions of manufacturers of cleaners and polishes; and the hospital and industrial products divisions of disposable paper products manufacturers.

In these companies, there is a clear distinction between consumer marketing and business to business PR techniques, though it can be argued that many of the same factors of quality, availability, price, brand name and value are at play.

The B to B – as it is increasingly known in jargon – public relations practitioner recognizes that he is supporting sales of "big ticket" items. It might be equipment costing thousands or, in the case of aircraft, millions of dollars in a single sale. Or it might be a contract for Kleenex at the Ford Motor company facilities, which will cumulatively involve an equally large amount. PR techniques to sell Kleenex to a large company will be different from those used to promote Kleenex to millions of consumers buying one or two boxes at a time.

The key messages in B to B PR must be relevant to the business buyer and are invariably concerned with cost, reliability in the case of equipment, service to ensure the minimum of down time, and, in some cases, the improvement of morale and productivity of the workplace. In many cases, B to B companies position themselves as the expert in a given field, seeking to elevate themselves from being a mere manufacturer of products. Office furniture producers depict themselves as office planners and leaders in ergonomics. Office equipment suppliers such as Xerox position themselves as expert consultants in work flows and document production.

■ Basic Techniques of B to B Public Relations

The first step, as with any PR or marketing communications task, is Target Identification. The exercise, conducted in association with others engaged in the marketing and sales function, will yield three crucial sets of information: the most important industries that are potential buyers of your products or services; the principal qualities, and the usual process of influence and decision making.

With the target audiences identified, you will be able to build a relevant media database.

You will also be able to plan for a broad-scale series of news announcements with the widest possible outreach and highly focused activities such as the following:

*   *Case histories.* Usually the most powerful and persuasive tool in this field, a detailed case study has multiple uses: an article in a trade journal, a newsletter to potential customers, an aid for the sales force. It is researched and produced in cooperation with a satisfied buyer/user of your product or service and should cover

cost savings, efficiency and other benefits. If you identify several industries as the biggest users of your products, plan to issue one case study on a monthly basis, each time on a different industry, to ensure maximum exposure.

- *Seminars.* Plan events to which media and potential customers can be invited to discuss some "hot" topic, with keynote speakers as magnets and a display or exhibition that demonstrates the products in use.
- *Speaking platforms.* Arrange for senior members of your staff to speak at industry conferences organized by the target groups you have identified.
- *Surveys.* When conducted among people working in your targeted industry groups, surveys can unlock media coverage, provide substance for customer mailings and newsletters, and become the central topic for seminars.
- *Sponsorships.* Your research will show which sporting or arts events will be attended by your specific target groups, offering opportunities for those all-important face-to-face meetings.
- *Scholarly initiatives.* Fund an annual lecture or a professorial chair at a major college or university that undertakes work related to your field or to your key customer groups. This will enhance your company image.

The combination of some or all of these initiatives, if done well, can confer the reputation of authority and thought leadership that is a cornerstone of successful B to B marketing.

■ Convergence

A phenomenon of the late 1990s is the discovery that the techniques of several specialties can be combined for more powerful marketing PR results that better meet the demands of a more sophisticated consumer. The following description is excerpted from an article by my colleague, Nancy Turett, managing director of Edelman Healthcare Worldwide; it first appeared in the October 1996 issue of *O'Dwyer's PR Services Report.*

> The health consumer is, first and foremost, a consumer. In addition to personal well-being, work, recreation, family, sex, and the future are all dimensions of the New Consumer's lifestyle. In the competition for share-of-mind, healthcare products and services are not just competing with each other; they are competing with Coca-Cola, Nike, Pizza Hut, and countless other consumer products and services.
>
> In the past, the marketing of healthcare products and services – from prescription medications to hospitals to medical devices – focused primarily on influencing health professionals, opinion leaders and health-oriented media. In some cases, messages were conveyed to target consumers, but in others the consumer never got the message – he or she just got the product in the form of a doctor's prescription.
>
> The "top down" view of how consumers are influenced, in which information flows in a one-way direction from the "influentials" to the media and ultimately, to the consumer, is no longer accurate.

A 1995 Yankelovich international analysis commissioned by Edelman Healthcare Worldwide found that consumers' confidence in traditional institutions – government, corporations, the media, healthcare providers – has eroded to an unparalleled degree. As a result, consumers are more self-reliant, and are driven to do their own information-gathering from an ever-growing list of resources, including the media, the Internet, and direct marketing, in order to make an informed purchasing decision.

Consumers are, themselves, the influentials. In many cases, it is the consumer who alerts the clinician to a novel treatment or new use for a medication that he or she has learned about from the media, the Internet, or direct marketing. Through advocacy groups, it is often consumers who are deciding where research dollars are spent, and increasingly, how the research should be conducted.

Harnessing the power of New Consumers requires far more than simply reaching them; it requires motivating and mobilizing them. The traditional healthcare marketing approach is not designed to achieve those goals.

Healthcare marketing today is increasingly calling for a melding of the creativity and mass appeal of traditional consumer marketing with the credibility and professional targeting associated with ethical pharmaceutical marketing.

This combination, which our firm calls Convergence Marketing, is an evolutionary, not revolutionary, approach. In addition to medical symposia and dissemination of materials to medical trade media, healthcare marketers should consider the approaches that have been most successful in the consumer public relations arena. For example, target publications for a new osteoporosis diagnostic device might include *Redbook*, for a new fertility drug they might include *GQ*, and for a cholesterol drug they might include *Bon Appetit*. A program venue could be a hotel or hospital health fair, but marketers should also open their eyes to other sites, including sports events, day care and senior centers, shopping malls and airports.

The "professional" audiences that influence consumers now reach far beyond doctors, nurses and pharmacists, and include coaches, hairstylists, mothers-in-law, travel agents, and so on. In addition, consumer advocacy groups have grown in number as well as influence, and building relationships with these opinion leaders now is as important as forging alliances with physician thought leaders.

New technology serves a dual purpose in efforts to reach the New Consumer. Computer games and surveys can be fun, attention-grabbing program tactics. On-line services, electronic bulletin boards and seminars, and Home Pages are powerful communications channels. However, marketers need to avoid the pitfall of shifting their focus completely to new technologies and the consumer. The health professional still needs to be respected and addressed. In this new era, successful healthcare marketing calls for a careful blending and balance of specialized industry knowledge and consumer marketing techniques.

■ Specialties by practice

Specialization in PR occurs in practice areas as well as by industry category. Important practice areas are Public Affairs, which includes public policy, governmental relations and legislative affairs; Environmental Affairs; Crisis and Issues Management; Employee Communications; Investor Relations; Corporate Identity and Reputation; Sponsorship and Event Management. Such practices can span a wide range of industries and organizations but, increasingly, individuals and agencies conduct their practice in a single industry or a small number of related industries.

Some of these specialties are discussed in greater detail in other chapters of this book, for example:

Corporate Reputation stands at the apex of all communications activity and requires the greatest breadth of knowledge of all the public relations specialties and the ability to orchestrate them to the benefit of the corporation's standing with its key audiences.

Crisis and Issues Management is covered in the chapters on Issue Identification and Management and Crisis and Catastrophe Communications, chapters 8 and 9.

Litigation public relations is a new specialty that has grown very quickly in the past decade; it is a 'first cousin' of crisis management and can be seen at work in some of the case studies featured in chapter 9. In this arena, PR specialists work closely with not only their clients but also their legal counsel because an issue has escalated to the point where it is going to be litigated in court. While the task of the lawyers is to achieve a favorable result before judge and jury (if one is involved), the PR practitioner has the job of ensuring that his client gets the right verdict in the "court of public opinion". While an important goal in itself, public opinion can also influence the courtroom result.

Investor Relations is touched on in an earlier section of this chapter, under the umbrella of financial public relations, where it can equally be considered a sub-specialty.

Sponsorship and Event Management has it own chapter (11) titled "Sponsorship? Philanthropy? Or Promotion?", and Public Affairs is covered in chapter 10.

■ Employee communications

Anyone contemplating a career in this well-defined communications specialty should consult some of the many books that have been written on the subject.

I hold particular views about employee communications. First, I find it offensive to see "employees" listed among consumers, lawmakers and others in the Target Audiences section of many PR plans. The employees to me *are* the company and as such deserve privileged treatment. This means that, insofar as law and regulations allow, they should be the very first to know of any development that is going to affect the company – good or bad.

This should be enshrined in every communications plan.

In fact, in most companies employee communications are the province of the personnel department, now often referred to as the Human Resources (HR) department, whose very name suggests placing human beings in the same category as coal, steel, wheat or money – just one of the raw materials needed to feed the machinery of business. To serve the information needs of HR, public relations people become functional assistants who help draft messages, prepare videos, write speeches and, possibly, produce the employee newspaper or magazine. In truth, there should be exceptionally close cooperation between the two disciplines of internal and external communications in any organization, regardless of the management reporting lines.

Employees are influenced as much by what they read in the media about their company and its place in its market and by the echo they get from their friends and acquaintances.

And a company's external audiences are greatly influenced, especially at the local and regional level, by the attitude of the employees who are the first-line ambassadors for their employers. If employees are confident and persuaded of the correctness of their company's position, they will convey their attitude with strength to the external audiences.

Although good employee relations built upon consistent, truthful communications should be the aim of any organization at all times, they are especially important in this current business climate.

Change Management, usually a kindly euphemism for job reductions, involves a large measure of employee communications and the pace of change in most countries is breathtaking. With the USA in the lead, Europe has been following close behind. Japan and Korea are changing with the bursting of the "bubble economy" and even the hallowed concept of jobs for life is now being questioned.

Mergers and Acquisitions have been taking place at unprecedented speed during the nineties, bringing change in their wake and exceptional challenges for those specializing in employee communications, as they seek to meld the different cultures, procedures and philosophies of two different merging companies. And the trend towards mergers and the creation of larger corporations is matched by the counter trend of divestiture and de-merger. One recent example was the "trivestiture" of AT&T, one of the world's largest corporations into three companies: AT&T which continues to offer telephone and wireless communications service to 70,000,000 subscribers, Lucent Technologies which manufactures the equipment used in telephony and NCR, maker of computers, scanners, automated teller machines (ATMs) and the card reading and pricing technology used in retail stores and supermarkets – the descendants of the original cash register made by the company more than 100 years ago. Another was the break-up of the Hanson Trust, the UK-based conglomerate, into four units and the similar break-up of ITT.

Diversity programs in America and many other countries with diverse workforces – by gender, race or religion – call for the most skillfully executed employee communications. In the USA particularly the need is accentuated by the epidemic of law suits brought by employees who claim they have suffered discrimination in hiring practices or have not had opportunity for promotion.

For the employee communications specialist and the Chief Communications Officer, it is now essential to learn how to manage within a changing economy and work environment and how to manage the change itself. These days, with constantly changing technology making certain jobs – and industries – outmoded overnight and a general shift from manufacturing to the service industries in the mature nations, the luxury of stability and security, mainstays of employee communication programs in the past, no longer apply. They must also learn how to balance the different messages directed at external audiences and those for internal consumption.

While the inflexible rule is that all messages must be truthful and cannot be altered (even though they may be slanted, or spun) for different target groups, those groups might react in widely differing ways.

Thus when a company announces significant staff reductions to keep costs under control there is likely to be dismay and anger among employees, and joy in the investment communities of Wall Street, the City of London, Hong Kong, Tokyo and the world's other financial centers. When the payroll goes down, the share price goes up. At times such as these, intense, careful, caring and honest communication with employees is of vital importance.

Companies that have established systematic, regular vehicles for employee communication in normal times are usually better prepared to cope when crisis or change occurs. The messages might change but at least the channels of communication are in place. A sudden uncharacteristic burst of communication using previously unseen vehicles usually does nothing more than heighten the sense of alarm and disbelief in the internal audience.

What are these vehicles? Here is a list of some of the tried and true. Organizations need not use all of them. Only the first is important for *all*; one or two of the others should be used regularly and will quickly establish themselves as the accepted means of communication.

* *Personal contact* is the most important and original means of communication with employees. Every other form is a substitute seeking to replace the easygoing dialogue that takes place between the boss and the staff that is normal in start-up companies and small businesses. Take every opportunity (no, *make* every opportunity) for the management to meet employees face to face in walkabouts, "town hall" meetings, conferences and the like. Fight off pressures from stay-at-home managers to avoid and postpone meetings at which they will have direct contact with employees.
* *Video*. Use video for the employee annual report, "state of the firm" messages sent out periodically. Video conferences are the next best thing to a personal visit.
* *News Posters* are ideal for companies with multi-locations.
* *E-mail and Intranet* are fast becoming the means of communication in many companies. They have the advantage of reaching all locations worldwide at the same time.
* *Parties* are great for team building.
* *Open Days* when staff and their families can visit the offices, factory, research laboratories, etc. of the organization are a proven way of reinforcing the commitment of employees and their families and a chance for them to see other facets of the operation beyond their own departments.
* *Newsletters and House Magazines* are the time-honored means of employee communication in most companies. They continue to be used nowadays for one reason: they work.
* *Hot Lines*: Recorded latest company news for anyone who wants to dial a special freephone number.

■ Specialization by function

The final form of public relations specialization is found in the various functional skills called for in PR departments or agencies. They are the communications techniques and tools used by the international PR practitioner to implement his strategies and concepts. Because they have the capability of delivering messages and information in very targeted forms, the specialties can reach specifically identified audiences as well as the general public. Companies have organized to create and deliver these tools, directly for corporate communications departments or as subcontractors to PR agencies.

Functional specialties in constant use by PR practitioners are:

- Publications, print production, graphic design
- Computer graphics
- Interactive communications, website development
- Video and film production and distribution
- Research
- Media tour planning and booking
- Advertisement creation, copywriting, layout, media planning
- Advertorial production
- Conference and event planning and management

CHAPTER 8

Issues Identification and Management

It is a source of wonderment to business leaders that companies held in high regard for their management, record of success and corporate citizenship can find themselves embroiled in highly publicized crises. The reputations of CEO and corporation so carefully nurtured are now suddenly imperiled and it all seems to come as a shocking surprise.

Globalization accentuates the potential for peril of a higher order, as issues manifest themselves in several countries at once and local conditions trigger problems not anticipated at headquarters. Crisis prevention is possible, and within the reach of the company public relations officer.

First, a simple definition of a crisis: It's an issue that has been poorly managed. On closer inspection, it becomes clear that, in the majority of such cases, there has been a trail of events or inaction over a period of several years or months, which has made the outcome almost a certainty. It should have been anything but a surprise to all who were close to the matter.

■ Foresee and forestall

An important part of the job specification of an organization's most senior public relations executive is to foresee and forestall any occurrence that could damage that organization's reputation, which he has been engaged to burnish.

Years of painstaking reputation-building can be wiped away in days or weeks if the company does not take early action to identify, intervene in and manage potentially damaging issues. It is just like a bank balance and the accumulation of capital, which take time and patience for most of us. Yet the savings account can quickly be wiped away by a risky investment on which our entire capital is wagered. It then becomes necessary to start the entire reputation-building task again, from the ground up – maybe from an even lower level, if credibility has been very severely damaged.

In the real world, unfortunately, it is often only when a crisis comes to trip up a company's management that thoughts turn to the measures that might have prevented the problem from reaching bursting point. Many are the corporate reputation management programs that were born in the furnace of post-crisis damage control.

The dynamics of issues management are not linear. They are circular and it is of little value to debate the chicken and egg problem of whether it takes a crisis to alert a company to the value of a disciplined issues management procedure or if the cycle begins with that procedure.

■ Cycle of action

The cycle of action with and without controls can be represented by a bisected circle in which proactive measures keep the company reputation well managed above the line and their absence sends it spinning into crisis below the line, as shown in chart 8.1 below:

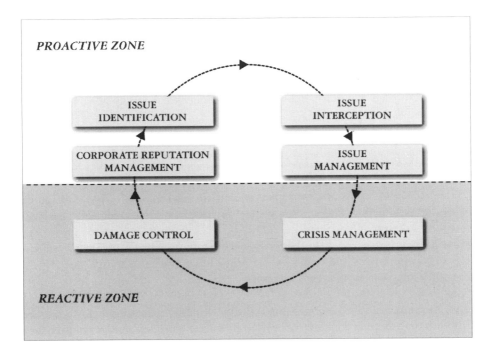

Chart 8.1

Obviously, the corporate aim must be to avoid moving into the bottom half of the circle, which I have termed the "reactive zone" to indicate that events and opponents are dictating your responses. A more colorful and provocative description, which I have eschewed, might be the "danger zone".

Assuming that the process begins with the commitment of the organization to undertake a conscious effort to achieve a high corporate reputation, the strategies and proactive initiatives adopted to meet that goal must be accompanied by comparable measures to ensure that all those efforts are not brought to naught by an inability to foresee where there are serious weaknesses.

■ Analogies

Sporting analogies abound when this topic becomes the subject of discussion at management meetings. For example, a participant may announce that, "A sound defense is as important as a great offense," or, "Let's put up lots of runs on the scoreboard to make sure we are unbeatable when the other team goes in to bat."

But business life does not operate by the rules of sportsmanship even though sports increasingly operate by the rules of business.

Analogies are all well and good to establish a rough-hewn point. In the world of reputation management, however, the opposing team doesn't always have to equal the score to inflict serious damage to the reputation of an organization.

Perhaps the boxing arena offers the most useful analogy. One contestant can control a fight for eight rounds and be ahead on points, with the championship in his grasp, but lose it through disqualification for delivering a low blow; the rival did not have to build a comparable score with referee and judges. Many a reputation has been demolished through stupidity, hubris, overconfidence or the risky notion that rule breaking will not be noticed.

■ Identification

Whether it begins as part of a proactive strategy formulated in a period of calm, or in the aftermath of a bruising crisis, a systematic process of issues identification is an important function of management and the professional public relations executives involved. That process should lead directly to the establishment of issues management, intervention initiatives and management procedures, which in most cases should prevent the "explosion" that ends in a crisis.

The tools for identification exist. They are in daily use among enlightened corporations in various countries around the world. But in most cases the topics are dealt with on a country-by-country basis and little attention is given to those issues which play out on a global or, at least, multi-country stage. Later in this chapter, I will recommend a methodical approach to identification of such issues, but there are also basic professional behaviors that are a "must".

■ Follow the news

The simplest advice is often the best: Public relations professionals must be avid readers of newspapers and magazines, and followers of radio and television programs. To these traditional media must now be added the Internet which is, arguably, the most international of all.

News and feature pages, current affairs and discussion programs should be closely followed. A sense of the news of the future must be developed, an understanding that a story just at its beginning could have an impact on your organization's business.

Make sure to listen occasionally to talk radio and carefully read letters to the editor and op-eds, those articles that appear opposite the daily editorials, in which people with various viewpoints express their opinions.

You should not rest there. Delve into lighter media fare – fashion, home and gossip columns, and situation comedies on television. Here more than anywhere, you will learn what is most important to people today.

Just reflect on the demise of the communist regimes of Eastern Europe. One of the most potent influences in that development was the increasing ability of residents behind the so-called Iron Curtain to receive foreign TV broadcasts. But it was not the rhetoric of politicians or commentators that weighed most heavily in shaping opinions of the opposing ideologies of capitalism and communism. It was the style of life depicted in the soaps, sitcoms, mysteries, variety shows and dramas that showed people that there was another way of living, materialistic maybe, but also with freedom of expression and the opportunity to mock authority without fear of retribution. They wanted to try this style of living as an alternative to what they had known before.

Such attention to the media will give you a good grasp of the current political, social and fashion context in which your organization is operating. It will allow you to assess opportunities and alert you to threats.

■ Parochial media

As someone who is responsible for international public relations, you must carefully select your regular newspaper reading and TV watching so that they provide you with more than simply a parochial view. Most media is extremely parochial. As a rule, the larger and more self-sufficient a country, the more locally focused is its media. Many American companies have grown to great size without needing to export, and their world view has therefore been minimized. Even for the largest American corporations which have operations around the world, in 180 or more countries, the home market of the USA remains preeminent and that colors the outlook of management. Very few American companies have reached a point at which they derive more than 50 per cent of their business from outside the USA. In turn, print and broadcast news media have reflected that inward look with modest foreign news and analysis.

On the other hand, in the smaller West European countries, corporate success requires global trading, companies are oriented to look beyond their national boundaries and the news media carry substantial international news. Consider Switzerland and Holland. Both these small countries are remarkable for the number of multinational corporations they have spawned. Yet, the "home" market for such companies' products is unlikely to exceed about ten per cent. Knowledge of the world and overseas markets is an essential prerequisite for anyone aspiring to a management position in these organizations. Media coverage of foreign affairs is correspondingly high in Swiss and Dutch media.

To round out your grasp of the issues making news around the globe, your reading list should include a well-written and eclectic weekly publication such as *The Economist*, and a couple of publications published domestically in the most important overseas markets for your organization. Listen to the BBC World Service and make sure you watch the news on CNN.

■ Surveys

The media is also an excellent resource to gain a more precise understanding of the issues of the day – and those of tomorrow.

Publishers, editors and TV program producers do not select topics for publication or airing merely on personal whim or instinct. They are guided by more formal research studies which tell them the topics of special concern to their readers and viewers at any given moment. So it is valuable to note the proportion of space or time devoted to various topics. The allocations will be instructive as to the topics of greatest interest to the public. While there are analytical services that will provide you with this data in certain countries, you can look in the media for more substantive information. Newspapers and magazines commission surveys on public attitudes and concerns, and publish the results. Often, these surveys set out to find out not only what views are held by the population but also the subjects that are of most concern to them.

The tempo of research invariably gathers pace during election seasons. The competing parties and the media seek to gauge the voters' priorities and views on a variety of matters, and cooperative research is commissioned from well-known research companies. Look carefully at this research, and tie it into your organization's areas of activity. You'll have more data than you can manage to interpret – and it is all free, if you know where and how to look.

The major research companies, among them Gallup, Opinion Research Corporation, Harris and Yankelovich, are eager publicity seekers and know that a sure-fire way to promote their names and services is to issue interesting research findings to the media. They go to great lengths to construct special research studies on current topics merely to engage the interest of editors. Editorial columns that contain data from these studies can be an invaluable free research resource.

Intelligent study of the media can, thus, provide you with rough bearings on a variety of attitudes you need to know, as you seek to zero in on those issues which might pose a threat to your organization. Possibly the information you glean will be sufficient for your purpose and you will have a very good idea not only of the issues of concern but also the ways in which they might be managed.

■ Risk management planning

But while sufficient for you personally, this data will almost certainly be insufficient for the senior management of your organization. This is especially the case if you feel certain issues are very serious and a significant budget, along with management time resources, needs to be allocated. Your management will almost certainly call for precise research data and a case strongly grounded in pragmatic business logic. Senior executives usually respond well to risk management planning. If you can clearly show the potential dangers involved in leaving an issue unmanaged, you will get the support and decision you need.

This is the time to consider commissioning a customized survey or participating in a standard caravan survey conducted regularly by one of the better research firms.

Every senior international public relations executive needs to be familiar with the multi-national research firms, their services and their regular caravan or cooperative studies. No research firm provides a global research capability based on its own staffing resources. But a number of firms offer controlled multi-country surveys, tailor-made for individual clients. Some offer surveys conducted on an annual basis or some other regular frequency.

■ Action plan and budget

Once you have prepared the way by showing credible and relevant research to your management, demonstrating that a threat exists, you will need to develop a realistic scenario. The penalties of inaction need to be described in concrete, not emotional, terms. Along with revealing existing threats, the study you have commissioned might also have uncovered opportunities for far-sighted preventive issues management and for production-related moves. If your organization has been the target of environmentalists seeking to close down factories of the type used by one of your operating divisions until they meet certain pollution requirements, you must now work with colleagues to assess not merely the damage to the company's reputation but also the real costs involved in factory closure. Get as close as you can to a realistic dollar figure that your company would have to pay for closure of the facility for one, three or six months, while the necessary new equipment or controls are installed. This figure will be the starting point for the creation of the issue management budget. If you can persuade your management that the preventive course of action will cost only a small percentage of the "worst case" scenario, you are likely to get approval for your proposal. Your plan, and its attendant costs, should cover any modifications to the factory as well as the costs of the communications component of the issue management program.

■ Government legislative agenda

An essential component of any issue identification plan is the monitoring of the legislative agenda for the immediate and longer-term future of each government in your organization's most important regions of activity. Government in this instance means authorities at the local, national and supra-national level, the last being, for example, the European Union. Nowadays, many policies and measures affecting multi-national businesses are made into law at the supra-national level.

Laws enacted by governments are important, but the regulations that follow, developed to interpret and enforce the intent of the laws, are always more important to business. They will dictate whether an organization has operated within or violated the law. Most problems arise in the fine print of regulations.

The legislative agenda is fairly easy to come by in democratic countries. Before elections, opposing political parties usually publish a manifesto which sets out their legislative priorities. When a government is formed, it, too, usually issues its agenda for each session of the parliament or congress. The full texts of manifestos can be obtained from the headquarters of the political parties, and the proposed legislative agenda is available at modest cost from the government publisher's office.

You can seek out reliable public affairs consultants who keep in close touch with political developments and undertake monitoring services on behalf of a variety of clients. They provide regular reports on changes in legislative priorities and also try to look ahead to the introduction of new bills that might affect your organization.

While some consultants and agencies confine their activities to monitoring, others offer services loosely described as lobbying, a process in which organizations can make sure their views are known and taken into account in the framing of new laws or regulations. (See chapter 10, Public Affairs.)

■ Pressure groups

The wellspring of most laws that have the potential to affect your organization is in the variety of pressure groups that abound in all full democracies.

These might have broad political agendas covering a range of issues – such as trade unions – or be dedicated to a single topic – such as the so-called pro-choice and pro-life groups in the conflict over legalized abortion in many countries.

It is easy to obtain written materials on the goals and proposals of pressure groups. Your remaining task is to assess the impact on your company if those goals are met and find their way into law.

Many pressure groups are broadly allied with political parties sympathetic to their ideals, and their leaders are often important figures within the hierarchy of those parties.

■ The Internet

The Internet has become a significant venue for issue identification and intervention. Its use for sharing and gathering information during times of crisis has increased in importance over the last two years, and it has become one of the most effective communications tools in the public relations professional's arsenal.

The Internet offers both new opportunities and challenges for communicating with and responding to an organization's publics. The dynamic nature of the medium makes it possible to share up-to-the-minute information instantly – and with little cost – to key audiences worldwide. The Internet also can pose challenges in the time of crisis or issue intervention, however, as it provides a global communications platform for adversaries and offers more information to which an organization must respond.

It can precipitate a crisis. Anything can be said, with little – if any – recourse. In addition, competitors can also use the Internet to communicate and manipulate the management of the issue/crisis situation.

There are three primary functions for which the Internet can be used in issue identification and intervention:

■ Monitoring Internet newsgroups and chats

Internet newsgroups and chats are often where an issue or crisis starts. In these open communication forums, Internet users discuss topics and potential issues that can brew to volatility. In some instances, issues arise on the Internet before the media becomes aware of them. For example, the Internet triggered a global crisis for Intel, manufacturer of the Pentium chip; an unhappy Pentium user posted Intel's unsatisfactory response to his complaint on the Internet and reached 20 to 30 million people around the world before any hint of the Pentium chip flaw appeared in the news media.

This "cyber crisis" eventually cost Intel and the computer industry not just lost sales and a potential replacement cost of $460 million but damaged credibility as well.

An Internet monitoring strategy is an important part of any issue identification and intervention plan. For example, monitoring relevant websites, newsgroups and chats allows an organization to conduct its own informal focus groups for continuous intelligence gathering and issue identification. On-line research capabilities grow daily. EEI-Online and NAMnet, for example, offer users daily, industry-specific data and reports. There are real-time, online links to major news and business wire services around the globe. Companies can identify trends and gain a perspective on the opinions of a sampling of the public, before those opinions enter the mainstream public arena. Internet monitoring allows an organization to stay in close touch with new developments, compare conflicting information and quell rumors and/or erroneous information.

■ Responding to Internet communications

In time of issue intervention or crisis, an organization may decide it is important to respond to what is being said online. In this situation, the organization has the opportunity to communicate directly with key constituencies and demonstrate a willingness to be forthright about addressing the issue.

If the organization decides this response is appropriate, it should disseminate information quickly and honestly. The organization should provide as much information as possible in a manner that will be easily understood by its constituencies. The information should be presented so that the public understands that the organization is interested in correcting inaccurate information that ultimately can be damaging to society.

This intervention or response can be implemented by posting information in Internet newsgroups, hosting a live chat session or even developing a website for ongoing dialogue.

■ Developing a website

In addition to responding ad hoc to what is being said in newsgroups or chats, an organization may decide to develop its own website as part of the issue identification and intervention plan. A website can provide the organization with an ongoing platform for communicating, and can help maintain a consistent flow of news to and from the online world. In addition, a website can help control the delivery of information. For example, posting a corporate statement, Q&A or relevant quotes can potentially decrease the amount of time spent speaking with journalists about the issue. Callers can be directed to the site to pull down the text.

Once a website is constructed, it is important to update it continuously over the course of the issue intervention. As soon as it is online, the website will become a source of information for consumers, journalists, and others. If it is ignored, the organization and its attempt to provide honest and forthright information will lose credibility.

Basic public relations tactics can complement the Internet as tools for issue identification and intervention. For example, third-party group representatives can be made available to interested publics via Internet chat sessions, Usenet newsgroups and/or mailing lists. Through such forums, key audiences can have access to credible "outside" spokespeople who can address questions about the issue or topic of concern.

■ Critical issues analysis

Visualize yourself now as the repository of a vast amount of data culled from a careful daily study and analysis of the media. You have reports of legislative proposals from your key regions around the world. You have a good sense of the demands being made by single- and multi-topic pressure groups, and you are watching the latest hot topics being debated in chat groups on the Internet.

But the mass of material is confusing and hard to bring into focus for the preparation of an international public relations plan and budget.

A methodology which I have termed "Critical Issues Analysis" (CIA) offers an orderly process. Its purpose is to prioritize the issues which have found their way onto your list and identify those of particular concern in several countries. CIA will thus deliver a prioritized shortlist of issues that are critical globally and allow you to develop centrally funded intervention and management strategies.

This is a vital preparatory stage in your PR planning process. It is relatively simple to do and it has the merit of involving executives – and therefore creating allies – in many countries and in different departments. Engaging in the process will pay huge dividends when you put forward your final public relations plan for approval; you will get the support and buy-in you need.

Here is how Critical Issues Analysis works.

STEP 1: List all the issues that you and your consultants around the world have identified as being sensitive for your organization. Do not be surprised if your first list has more than 50 issues, some of them closely related, one to the other.

STEP 2: Sort the issues into groups under a series of subject headings. Examples might be:

Social
Environmental
Personnel/human relations
Competition
Safety
Potentially harmful product ingredients

Shorten the list by combining similar issues into one.

STEP 3: Check the wording of each issue to ensure it will be easily understood by someone unfamiliar with the topic. Avoid jargon – it does not travel.

STEP 4: Make a list of senior public affairs and public relations executives in your organization's regional and national subsidiaries and affiliates. Add some names from among the top rank of executives in line operations and the office of the Chief Legal Officer. Add up to five names from among your most senior regional external consultants. By now, you will have a research universe of 20 or more names. Try not to have more than 25 names in total, as you embark on the next step.

STEP 5: Compose a letter to members of the research panel, asking each person to review the list of issues very carefully. Then ask the interviewees to rank each issue, on a scale of one to ten, one indicating that the issue is of minimal importance and ten signaling a hot-button issue needing maximum and urgent attention. Leave room for each respondent to add an important issue that might have been missed, or to comment on issues that he believes are cool now but have the potential to become hot in a year or two. It is the purpose of this exercise, after all, to identify those issues that are gathering speed and support. The letter should stress the importance of the exercise for the organization as a whole. It is usually a good idea to send it out over the signature of the CEO, to signal its priority.

STEP 6: Analyze the results by adding the scores given to each issue and review the comments added by the respondents. You will find that the issues divide themselves into four distinct categories:

- *Global*: Four to seven issues will be ranked high by all or a large majority of respondents, indicating a global threat. These are likely to have an average score in excess of seven.
- *Multi-country*: One or two issues are significant across several countries in a region.
- *Isolated*: Some issues score nine or ten in one or two markets.
- *Minimal*: Some issues are of minimal concern to all respondents (average score below four).

The comments may point to issues that are on the rise and thus will need more attention in your planning for the future.

The CIA should be conducted annually, as an essential preliminary to the development of the public relations and issues management plan. Those issues which achieve a high global score should be studied closely. Each should have a special mini-issue management plan written for it, and global financial and personnel resources should be applied. Issues that are significant in a particular region can be dealt with by a regional team and with a regional budget. Resources and guidance from corporate headquarters should be made available if needed. Similarly, single-country issues, even if they are serious, should be dealt with at the local level. However, it is possible that the country unit concerned lacks experience and resources. In such cases, global headquarters should assist in the form of strategic and program development, possibly assigning one or more executives on loan.

The methodical approach of Corporate Issues Analysis will provide a solid basis for the issues management recommendations you make to your CEO. Involve a representative selection of executives from within your organization as participants in the process, to ensure enthusiastic and committed implementation of the program.

CHAPTER 9

Crisis and Catastrophe Communications

There are ten kinds of crisis. Four of them are slow-burning issues, which can be detected and managed with the identification and intervention techniques discussed in the previous chapter:

- Litigation
- Product Liability
- Action by Pressure Groups
- Labor Disputes

The other six kinds of crisis usually come as surprises, even though most of them are potential hazards for all businesses. In all cases, advance preparation can limit the damage from such crises and ensure a prompt and effective response when they occur:

- Exposé or Whistle Blowing
- Hostile Takeover Bid
- Disclosure or Revelation
- Disaster/Accident/Explosion/Oil Spills
- Production Mistake, Product Recall
- Terrorism, Tampering, Extortion

■ Ten golden rules

Whether a slow-burning issue finally bursts into flames or a completely unforeseen catastrophe takes place, there are Ten Golden Rules to observe in times of crisis:

■ 1. The CEO takes charge

The chief executive officer must be informed of any *major* crisis *immediately*, wherever he is and whatever the time. The ultimate impact of the crisis on the company's reputation and bottom line is shaped in the first few hours after a "surprise" crisis occurs. Of course, Murphy's Law dictates that most crises occur on the evening before the start of a long weekend and the CEO has just boarded a 14-hour intercontinental flight. In such cases, his second-in-command must be told and he should assume responsibility.

The need for CEO involvement might appear obvious but it is not the rule in most companies, which pay dearly in the long run. When companies become bureaucratic and grow out of touch with their consumers and other audiences, they also tend to build walls around the senior management team and, in particular, the chief executive officer. He is shielded from activists, shareholders, customers and the general public. The media is seldom, if ever, provided open access.

In such companies, there is no recognition of the rule that it is vital for the CEO to take personal charge of every significant crisis and to go to the site of the crisis as fast as possible.

The importance of this rule prompts me to propose a new Law of Crisis Management: "The negative reputation impact of a crisis is directly proportionate to the length of time it takes for the CEO to assume control and reach the scene." The underpinning of this law is solid.

- Fritz Gerber, shortly after being elected Chairman and CEO of Hoffman-La Roche, in addition to his role as chief of Zurich Insurance, arrived at the scene of a factory accident at a company unit in France within 14 hours of its occurrence. There were several fatalities, but his prompt action and presence ensured that there was minimal negative publicity and no lasting hostility. Compare this with an earlier company accident that occurred at the Seveso, Italy, plant of Hoffman-La Roche's subsidiary Icmesa, before Gerber took over. A hexachlorophene production unit exploded, sending a cloud of dioxin into the air. Neither the chairman, Dr. Adolf Jann, nor any senior executive of Hoffman-La Roche, visited the site, in fear of being jailed by distraught Italian authorities, and Seveso became the symbol of industrial catastrophes for at least a decade within Europe. It was the subject of some 60 books, countless articles and TV documentaries. In fact, no deaths or serious long-term ill effects have been proven to have been the direct result of the explosion. Some believe the biggest casualties of the Seveso affair were Hoffman-La Roche's reputation and its bank balance, because millions were paid out to assuage the concerns of an anxious group of citizens and their local government.
- There have been many fatal air crashes, notwithstanding the fact that air is statistically safer than travel by land or water. One crash remains fresh in the memory of most people in Europe and America – that of Pan Am 103, which was brought down by a terrorist bomb over the village of Lockerbie in Scotland, on December 21, 1988. The chairman of Pan Am did not visit the site or the hospital to which injured survivors had been sent. It was left to the Queen of England to travel to Lockerbie, to offer sympathy and visit the injured in hospital. Pan Am is pursued to this day by a group of parents of children killed in the crash; the airline never recovered financially from the disaster and went into bankruptcy. In contrast Nicki Lauda was on the scene of a fatal crash of a Lauda Air 767 in Thailand and Michael Bishop, CEO of British Midland was at the site of a British Midland 737 crash at Kegworth within hours. Many credit Lauda's visit as critical to saving his airline.
- Of all the many disastrous oil spills that have caused severe environmental damage, the most notorious is the Exxon Valdez spill in Prudhoe Bay, Alaska, in 1989.

Probably no worse in reality than other, bigger spills, it is the emblem of how to superimpose a public relations debacle onto an environmental catastrophe. Exxon Valdez remains imprinted on the memory for the way in which communications in the first hours after the spill were bungled and because Exxon's chairman and CEO did not deign to visit the affected area.

- An explosion that killed more than 2,000 people at a chemical plant in Bhopal, India, in 1984, has gone on record as one of the worst peacetime disasters in this century. Yet the financial and reputation consequences for Union Carbide, the ultimate owner of the plant, were softened by the prompt and brave action of Warren M. Anderson, the CEO. Within hours, he flew to India to be among the victims, to start an investigation, open a fund for those affected, consult with the authorities and make sure emergency relief services were operating efficiently. It surely needed courage to resist the temptation to say that the company operating the Bhopal plant was an autonomous subsidiary and to confront the prospect of being arrested and jailed. Instead, this single action did much to maintain Union Carbide's reputation, when many of the circumstances of the explosion seemed to point to quite inadequate management oversight of equipment and safety measures in the manufacturing process at the local facility.

Before becoming too critical of corporate leaders who did not act – and travel – promptly, one should understand the powerful corporate dynamics that might have worked against their direct involvement. In many major bureaucratic corporations, there are legions of executives who see their roles as shields for their senior management. They talk about "crisis containment", a valid policy, but only when directed by the CEO himself, in which the first battles are fought by the lower ranks. Such executives prevent travel by the CEO by saying, "Your place as captain is here on the bridge of the ship, directing operations. How can you do that if you are at the scene of the battle?"

Ploys like these ought not to work with high-caliber CEOs, who trust their own judgment and reject late, staff-screened data that may minimize the damage that a catastrophe might cause.

The top-flight CEO will know instantly what to do. If he has the advice of a strong, honest public relations advisor, all the better. Job number one will be to get to the scene of the disaster where a command post can be set up. The CEO should never be seen in a TV interview in a wood-paneled office, behind a large desk, while television news crews are showing pictures of the injured or body bags containing the fatalities.

Having taken charge, the CEO's next step is to execute Golden Rule No. 2:

■ 2. Issue holding statement within two hours

Two hours is the maximum length of time that should pass before you issue a statement summarizing the facts of the matter as far as they are known. Stick to the facts and do not elaborate or try to interpret them. In the case of an oil spill, air or rail crash, explosion or other accident, the media will begin its coverage immediately. Every minute you delay with your statement means reporters must find alternative "experts" to explain the cause. Corporate and industry enemies will be eager to step in and give their views.

Speculation far from the truth might well take hold in the public mind and become the reality before you even start to communicate.

I cannot move on without citing the famous quotation of Winston Churchill that acts as a caution to all public relations practitioners: "A rumor can be half way round the world before the truth has time to get its trousers on." It is amazing to realize that this was said years before satellite TV and the Internet, although that powerful often-overlooked medium, radio, had been in existence for several years.

The initial statement should be open, sympathetic toward any victims, but brief. It is perfectly acceptable to state that the cause of the problem is not known, along with giving assurances that everything is being done to find out. The statement should end with the time and place of the next update to the media, setting the scene for a regular dialogue during the crisis period.

■ 3. Create a crisis task force

In any significant crisis, the CEO should nominate a special task force early. The task-force leader should be a senior executive of the company, who will be able to take on some of the time-consuming communication duties that will emerge as the crisis evolves. The task force should consist of a legal representative, a communications officer and the technical specialists appropriate to the accident.

Members of the task force should be assigned full time in the heat of the crisis, with counsel and support from a specialist PR agency team. The secondary effects of a crisis can be extremely damaging and the huge time demands it creates distract the company and its executives from their true purpose. The company must field two teams, defense and offense, at the same time. The role of the communications officer is to ensure that the media and other audiences who have a right or a need to know are kept informed at regular intervals.

In some catastrophes, a secondary crisis is created as a result of inadequate communications to specific groups. In the 1996 case of TWA 800, when a Boeing exploded in midair and crashed in New York's Long Island Sound without any survivors, media coverage turned at one stage, from the investigation of the cause of the crash and the location and identification of the bodies, to complaints from relatives of the passengers who said they were being given inadequate information and were being poorly treated by TWA.

■ 4. Establish a press office within six hours

The task force communications officer should set up a fully staffed and equipped press office within six hours of the first news of the crisis. It should be separate, with phone and fax numbers different from those in the regular company press office. All incoming calls from media inquiring about the crisis must be routed to this center. All other staff should be told they should not speak to the media.

The staffing of the news bureau/press office should be sufficient to cope with the intensity of media interest. On-site skills should include:

- Ability to create and update a special "crisis news" page on the company website.
- Capacity to log all media inquiries and organize them by topic so that Q&A templates can be prepared.
- Specialist ability to deal with the requirements of the electronic media. The designated professional should also be responsible for the preparation and dissemination of company-produced video B-roll and video news releases.
- Support-staff capability to undertake time-consuming administrative tasks involved in disseminating statements, calling back all media who have made requests for specific kinds of information when it becomes available, and all the other detail work that is vital to establishing an effective two-way channel.

The communications officer must also make sure that, if any potentially damaging evidence emerges, he is the one to inform the media, however distasteful or unwelcome the task. The result will be much less damaging than if the facts come to light from another source.

■ 5. Arrange brief media training refresher course

Although the CEO and other senior executives have probably undertaken media training previously, it is a "must" to arrange a short refresher course – even if only for an hour or two – to remind your spokespersons of the tenets of a successful interview and to rehearse them on the key messages to be communicated, along with answers to likely questions.

■ 6. Call on civic and other government leaders for help

In cases of loss of life, property and similar dangerous situations, do not try to fight the crisis alone. Call on civic, police and other appropriate leaders for help. Not only will this help to mitigate the disaster more quickly, it will make the impact of the crisis a shared problem. Often companies are the co-victims in an "act of God" crisis but all too often they get positioned as blameworthy (or at least suspect) while others suffer.

■ 7. Announce establishment of a disaster fund within 24 hours

The victims of some disasters are faced with immediate, unusual expenses for medical treatment, travel and shelter, and often have no money to cover these costs. Many companies involved in crises suffer additional reputation damage because it takes a long time to establish a fund to deal with victims' costs. Even when a fund has been set up, it can take years for the money to be released to those in need. Damage from the crisis can be reduced by the creation of an emergency crisis fund to take care of immediate expenses – without red tape – of those people who have suffered. Prompt action in disbursing the money when it is actually needed creates goodwill that will surely be reflected in the company's reputation and the financial settlements that are ultimately made.

■ 8. Institute daily news conferences

Establish a routine in the immediate aftermath of a crisis that reflects the news-gathering needs of the media but also allows the press center to operate efficiently. By scheduling a daily news conference to provide progress reports at a time that fits in with deadlines, press officers can respond publicly to a variety of media inquiries and extend an invitation to participate in the next press briefing when there will be a Q&A session. This system ensures that *all* media are equally well served and no favorites are given exclusive treatment, something that would be guaranteed to alienate the majority of reporters.

■ 9. Communicate proactively

In the pressure of a crisis situation, it is easy to become reactive under the onslaught of media attention and questioning. Yet it is vital for successful crisis management that you take control and communicate proactively. Do not wait for questions to be asked. In addition to the daily news conference, make sure you release regular news bulletins – by fax, video news release, web page and all the other means at your disposal. Report what you have found out about the cause of the crisis, what the company is doing to put things right, how it is helping those affected, and steps being taken to prevent future occurrences.

■ 10. Survey public opinion

Do not fly blind in a crisis. Opinions may vary among senior management as to the extent of public awareness of the crisis and its effect on your company's reputation. The impact of the crisis will also vary widely in different parts of the world. You should know at intervals how your response to the crisis is being viewed by employees and audiences key to your business, for example, opinion leaders and members of the public.

So one early step should be the commissioning of a series of surveys which will give you the information you need. The feedback will help you to adjust your communications strategies and will also tell you where the crisis has had the most impact. Although the Internet and satellite television transmission mean that news gets around the world in an instant, it does not follow that all parts of the world and local media will be interested in your crisis. Most media is extremely parochial and, unless there is a direct, local connection, will not report even on significant events taking place far away. The Seveso hexachlorophene plant explosion was a top news item in Europe for a decade, but it went unnoticed in the USA. Similarly, Shell's Brent Spar Oil Rig brouhaha with Greenpeace was headline news and high on the political agenda throughout Europe for several months, and was followed with interest in certain other countries. However, in the USA and Latin America, the media focus was on other problems nearer to home and if anyone there had heard of Brent Spar, it was unlikely to be damaging to Shell Oil's reputation.

Catastrophes and emergencies are not exclusively reserved for poorly managed and ill-prepared companies. They can affect all.

■ Being prepared

The company that systematically identifies issues early on, then manages them purposefully, will dramatically reduce the potential of being surprised by a crisis. If that company prepares itself to expect the unexpected, it will be at the ready to face a crisis when it does occur.

Finally, if the ten golden rules are followed, the company will control damage to its reputation and set the stage for a strong recovery program.

Crises are among the best-documented specialties of public relations, perhaps because they so often capture the headlines, much to the chagrin of the organizations concerned. The most useful way to illustrate various types of crisis is through cases covering both slow-burning issues and surprises. You will, however, never have heard about some of the most adroitly handled crises precisely because they attracted little attention in the media. The companies involved are not usually eager to publicize the steps they took to manage the crisis because it would work against the achievement of the goal: containment of the problem to the most limited audience possible.

For the sake of illustrating crisis management, following are some landmark cases.

■ Dow silicone breast implant litigation

In the 1980s, when isolated stories began to surface about the ills of women with silicone breast implants, Dow Chemical Corporation was already the veteran of a monumental crisis. It had been the manufacturer of Agent Orange, infamous as a defoliant in Vietnam combat and later associated with cancer in veterans and birth defects in their children. Now the company was being pulled to the center of a target board again, because decades earlier it had conducted toxicological tests of silicone, used in breast implants made by Dow Corning, Inc., a joint venture owned by Dow Chemical and Corning, Inc. Instead of veterans suffering the lingering effects of exposure to Agent Orange, it was thousands of women with breast implants, complaining of a variety of illnesses they attributed to the implants.

Plaintiffs and their attorneys argued that Dow Chemical, though not the manufacturer of the implants, was liable because it had conducted the tests that showed the possibility of health problems from silicone implants and had concealed that fact to sustain sales and credibility. The news media gave elaborate coverage to mounting anecdotal evidence about women's illnesses. Plastic surgeons had eagerly participated in the marketing of implants as figure enhancements, without warning patients of the risks involved, including rupture or leakage. The product initially had not had to pass Food and Drug Administration tests for safety, which became required only in 1976.

Responding to first stages of the crisis, when evidence began piling up and panic spread to thousands of women, neither Dow Chemical nor Dow Corning seemed especially sympathetic toward the ailing women. Denial of responsibility was the operative strategy.

In a 1984 decision in San Francisco, Dow Corning was ordered to pay $1.7 million in punitive damages to a plaintiff. During the appeals process, a secret settlement was reached and all court documents, including Dow Corning records, were sealed from further scrutiny.

By the end of 1991, not only had the FDA issued a rule requiring breast implant makers to submit approval applications but a California jury had awarded a woman $7.3 million in damages when she successfully associated her symptoms of auto-immune disease with her Dow Corning implants.

■ FDA moratorium

Early in 1992, the FDA put a moratorium on further sales of silicone breast implants and within months Dow Corning, the dominant company in the implant business, stopped manufacturing them, nonetheless denying possible harm. The FDA then lifted the ban but restricted the use of the implants to women willing to participate in clinical studies.

By 1995, Dow Corning, once the manufacturer of some 5,000 products, had filed for bankruptcy reorganization. It faced tens of thousands of lawsuits. A $4.2 billion fund for global settlement of consolidated suits offered in 1994 by Dow Corning and other manufacturers had fallen apart when hundreds of thousands of claims exceeded the potential resources of the fund. Once Dow Corning filed for bankruptcy reorganization, the other defendants in the suits, including Minnesota Mining and Manufacturing (3M), Bristol-Myers Squibb and Baxter, constructed a separate fund plan.

A dramatic component of the evolution of the crisis was the nature of corporate response. Dow Corning had historically answered to its two parents, Dow Chemical and Corning, rather than to a marketplace, as it grew to huge success based on applications of silicone compound. When silicone implants were launched in 1963, they had required no FDA review and were said to be seen as safe by company chemists. Breast augmentation became popular. Under pressure from competitors, a dozen years later, Dow Corning developed new silicone-based implants in a hurry, allegedly ignoring internal and scientific concerns that the products were prone to leakage and rupture.

Ms. magazine ran an article reporting implant problems that had been discussed in medical journals and inveighing against big-breast culture. This elicited a response from Dow Corning that passed responsibility to physicians. Not until 1984 did the company focus on the problem seriously, having by now been found guilty in the first breast implant case to go to trial – the San Francisco decision of $1.7 million in damages, for selling a poorly designed product with a manufacturing defect. Much incriminating evidence had been discovered among 200 unsorted boxes of documents Dow Corning reluctantly turned over in response to the plaintiff's request.

■ Secret settlement

Following the secret settlement and sealing of documents, the company did not launch any research or express any concern for women who might have had problems with implants. But it did update a marketing brochure to include possible adverse reactions to implants.

That Dow Corning was the offspring of Dow Chemical and the Agent Orange history, itself replete with insensitivity and arrogance, did not help. The company had emerged from that case with an overdraft at the "goodwill" bank and had no reserves to draw on.

Women with problems associated with implants began to organize for support and lobbying activity; a consumer activist group sued the FDA to release implant safety studies provided by Dow Corning, and a US District Court judge ordered them made public.

The spark that ignited flames of panic across the USA, however, was a CBS-TV "Face to Face with Connie Chung" program on women with breast implants who had suffered health problems. Incidents came to light as the media discovered more victims with heart-rending stories to tell. Local and national media got into the act, and business publications took Dow Corning to task, especially after the sealed documents of the 1984 case were leaked. A Business Week story in 1991 charged that the company had known for more than a decade of animal studies linking implants to cancer and other illnesses.

It was ironic that the wife of a Dow Corning executive responsible for the company's ethics program concluded in 1990 that her implants were the source of her medical problems; her husband observed that the company had failed in its responsibilities to do further tests, produce records and issue warnings. He would eventually tell what he knew to *Business Week* and that story would lead to a book, *Informed Consent*, by reporter John Byrne. When the curtain was lifted off the inner workings of the company, it became obvious that its attorneys had won battles with its reputation managers, advocating continued production of implants and denial of responsibility.

Following the 1991 award in California of $7.3 million to a plaintiff, and a finding that Dow Corning was guilty of fraud, some members of Congress joined the Dow antagonists. An FDA task force found Dow Corning clinical studies weak and ineffective in assuring safety.

And still, company communications condemned the legal process, the politicization of the issue and sensational media coverage, with no sympathy for victim complaints. This, despite the crisis communications counsel of Burson-Marsteller.

A Texas law firm and public relations agency launched a practice specializing in handling breast implant litigation. They quickly attracted 2,500 clients and plenty of media coverage.

Soon after the early 1992 FDA moratorium on sales of silicone gel implants, a new Dow Corning CEO initiated a turnaround in media relations and document disclosure, but it was clearly too late. He announced two months later that Dow Corning was ending its breast implant business. Within a year, there were nearly 10,000 suits against Dow Corning.

In the first trial against Dow Chemical, in 1995 in Reno, Nevada, the company, because of its involvement testing silicone gel for Dow Corning, was found guilty of conspiracy to commit fraudulent concealment and was ordered to pay $14 million in damages to the plaintiff.

Another 13,000 suits against Dow Chemical were next in line.

After Dow Corning filed for bankruptcy protection, it was still on the attack; an article by its CEO condemning "The Tort Monster that Ate Dow Corning" appeared in the *Wall Street Journal*.

The essence of his message had merit. Journalists began to question whether they had been misled by overly zealous plaintiffs' attorneys, quick to accuse, poor in scientific backup. First to question media gullibility was the influential *New York Times* medical reporter, Gina Kolata. Then came ABC-TV's *Nightline*, *Fortune* and others, who criticized the media's readiness to run with sensational, anecdotal stories, scarcely stopping to find scientific evidence.

In the courts, Dow Chemical had become the deep-pocketed target, now that Dow Corning had left the field, and verdicts went against it. In mid-1996, there were 13,000 remaining breast implant suits against Dow Chemical, which had the potential to drive that company into bankruptcy, too.

New medical studies, however, were yielding results that questioned the link between implants and cancer and auto-immune disease, though links still were seen with connective-tissue diseases.

By 1996, Dow Chemical, counseled by Ketchum Public Relations, was including in corporate communications expressions of sympathy for the affected women. Observers were seeing more evidence of crisis management strategies in the company's corporate behavior than had been the case at Dow Corning.

■ Junk science

The issue of "junk science" came forward. In an Oregon case at the end of 1996, a US District judge ruled that scientific evidence that implants cause disease was too unreliable to be presented to a jury. In another late-1996 move, Dow Corning offered a new plan for paying creditors, predicated on a "science trial" to show whether there is any scientific basis for contentions that silicone from ruptured or leaking implants causes diseases.

The crisis had cooled somewhat. But corporate survival and damage to corporate reputation are still at stake.

■ PruBache litigation

When there is no proactive communications process in place to target both internal and external audiences, the impact of a crisis becomes considerably more severe, as was the case with Prudential Bache Securities in the 1980s, an example of a litigation crisis turbocharged by a surprise factor – evidence from a group of employee whistle blowers.

The venerable, rock-solid Prudential Insurance Co. of America, whose Rock of Gibraltar logo was strewn liberally through its product and subsidiary-company images, took the risky road rather than the high road in 1981 by acquiring a troubled brokerage company, Bache and Co. The object: to launch cradle-to-grave financial service capabilities, and take advantage of tax reform legislation and regulations that encouraged creativity in tax shelters.

What resulted instead, within the decade, was the destruction of Prudential's reputation, as the new company undertook the aggressive sale of limited partnerships, for example in real estate and energy. It promised investors the benefits of tax shelters, income yield and a hedge against inflation. The venture was doomed. Trading on the Prudential's history of conducting safe, secure insurance business, PruBache pushed low-quality investment products hyped by false claims, through a sales force that either did not care or was pressured into unethical behavior. More than $8 billion of risky partnerships were sold; thousands of lives and careers were ruined; homes, retirement funds, college educations were lost; lawsuits started, not against the new venture but against the deep-pocketed parent company.

Meanwhile, Prudential Insurance had also become the subject of an investigation into allegations of churning accounts in 28 states – agents selling new and larger policies on a trade-in basis from older policies whose dividends, the agents said, would pay the premiums of the new policies. Policy holders who believed the deal ultimately found the premiums were exhausted, heavy cash input was necessary and new premiums were substantially higher.

Rogue agents had done the deed, Prudential officials said, firing 500.

■ Consolidation

Further criticism of Prudential resulted when chairman Arthur Ryan encouraged New Jersey, where the company is headquartered, to lead consolidation of state investigations into allegations of churning life insurance policies. Critics were quoted in a page-one story in the *New York Times* early in 1997, claiming that state regulators had gone easy on Prudential because it is not only New Jersey's third largest employer but its executives have historically provided financial support for politicians and their pet projects, and have been close advisors to governors and others in high posts. Not enough, critics said of the New-Jersey-led decision that Prudential agents were guilty as accused and that the company should be fined $35 million and sign a settlement of at least $410 million for wronged policy holders. The challenge to the settlement went to Federal District Court, with the likelihood of a continuing stream of reporting on the seemingly endless saga.

Then came a whistle-blowers' suit, with former sales managers charging that they had been disciplined and finally fired when they tried to stop churning practices.

In what was called the costliest scandal in the history of Wall Street, Prudential admitted charges of fraud in 1994 to avoid criminal indictment and began settling $1 billion in claims. Media coverage was intensive, starting with the initial revelations of fraud by the *New York Times* reporter Kurt Eichenwald, who later wrote a well-regarded book on the company's problems, *The Serpent on the Rock*.

As a slow-moving, bureaucratic, out-of-touch organization set about its metamorphosis and internal clean-up, a new chief communications officer arrived. Elizabeth Krupnick found devastated employees who'd had to read about their employer's behavior in newspapers, had received poor, jargon-laden communications from management, and had far worse perceptions of Prudential than did outside publics.

■ Inconsistency

All publics also had to be addressed, to restore the confidence of investors, policy-holders, ratings agencies and the Wall Street community. The company's inconsistent visual representation – a stylized rock image here, a subsidiary's obscure name there – was examined and streamlined by corporate identity specialists Siegel & Gale. Advertising agency Fallon McElligott came on board to create a new campaign that would leverage the 100-year-old Rock icon, yet deliver a contemporary, dynamic message. Print ads starred somewhat older, real people, who had taken rock-solid control of their lives and achieved financial stability.

Public relations staffers who had simply responded to media inquiries now took on more proactive approaches to corporate communications. Technology was introduced – electronic mail, an intranet system, interactive sales tools and a website for closer relationships with customers. Two community relations campaigns were launched. The Spirit of Community Awards go to youngsters who take community service seriously and to high school journalists who cover youth community service; the program also includes a youth leadership training component. The Helping Hearts Program makes matching grants to volunteer emergency medical service squads for portable cardiac defibrillators.

There's a long way to go for Prudential to restore its ravaged reputation. Creative, strategically-driven communications work is a major player in the effort, but the company is fighting against heavy odds. Month by month, there are new reports from courts that have handed down guilty verdicts to the Pru, along with fines, each in the tens of millions of dollars. And in each report, there is a retelling of the unethical behavior of some of its employees in this dark period of its history.

■ Nestlé boycott

When a British journalist suggested publicly in 1974 that hard-selling manufacturers of powdered infant formula were contributing to the deaths of Third World infants, he found a ready audience among a new breed of activists – anti-business groups, religious organizations, champions of Third World concerns and an end to world hunger, and feminists. The product, he said, encouraged poor, illiterate mothers to give up breast feeding in favor of the heavily advertised powder. They often diluted it excessively to make it go further and used dirty water and unsanitary procedures – all of which led to deadly digestive disorders and malnutrition in their babies. The author recognized that some mothers were malnourished themselves and could not breast feed adequately, while others had to take employment to support their families and had to use supplements to breast milk.

Even though several infant formula manufacturers operated in the Third World, the booklet the author had written was soon reprinted without the qualifications and with the title, *The Baby Killers*, by the Swiss activist Third World Working Group. In quick succession, these developments occurred: Nestlé sued for libel in the Swiss courts, wrongly assuming that a legal victory would resolve the problems of public perception. The result was that the assertions made in the book received a second, unexpected burst of publicity as evidence was given during the hearings. And although the judge found that Nestlé had indeed been libeled, technically, he awarded Nestlé a derisory 1/2 cent in damages, the lowest amount possible, and accompanied it with a lengthy judicial statement that made it clear he felt the company morally and ethically guilty.

One result was that INFACT, the Infant Formula Action Coalition, was established in the USA, focusing primarily on Nestlé and organizing a world boycott of Nestlé products, with such slogans as "Crunch Nestlé Quick", punning on the brand names of Nestlé chocolate products.

■ Religious coalition

Boycott leaders were not concerned that the US Nestlé company did not sell infant formula. They were soon joined by The World Council of Churches, national Protestant and Catholic institutions and local churches, teachers' unions and other labor groups, and Hollywood celebrities. Soon media attention turned to other major manufacturers of infant formula: Glaxo in the UK and Ross Laboratories (subsidiary of Abbott Laboratories), Bristol-Myers, and Wyeth Laboratories in the USA, along with a producer based in Holland.

But the main media spotlight remained focused on the Swiss company. Nestlé at its headquarters in Switzerland became the leader of an industry group that took an uncompromising position, emphasizing that its advertising always stressed that breast milk is best; powdered formula actually saved infants' lives; local sales people were vital educators of mothers on infant care; distribution of samples to new mothers through hospitals was generous and educational rather than a marketing ploy; and government authorities welcomed the manufacturers' activities. The industry alliance was ICIFI, the International Council of the Infant Formula Industry.

The media had a field day, locally, nationally and internationally, especially if a celebrity joined the ranks of the boycotters. Publicity-savvy groups often called press conferences to announce they had uncovered another piece of evidence about Nestlé's aggressive marketing in a Third World country, where tactics were used that were even outside the company's long-standing sales and marketing guidelines.

It should be specially noted by those who work in decentralized multinational organizations that the "violations" uncovered by the coalition were in most cases the work of sales agents who did not even belong to Nestlé and a few that arose from the activities of "rogue", distant local subsidiaries. Thus, a fine company, practicing the virtues of empowering local management and agents to operate entrepreneurially and independently, paid a high price for their mistakes or excesses. In the matter of corporate reputation, a company is as strong as its weakest link.

At headquarters in Vevey, Switzerland, and at Nestlé USA, executives insisted the boycott was having no impact on sales. The US company designated senior staffers from several unrelated departments to constitute truth squads that were trained to face off with adversaries in venues across the country.

Edelman Public Relations was hired in the US and London, to work with Nestlé USA and the international formula manufacturers' organization to correct misinformation in media coverage. The mission also included educating groups within the adversary coalitions about Nestlé's historic efforts to improve Third World nutrition through research, and a charge to effect a positive outcome to the landmark World Health Organization conference convened in Geneva in 1979 to act on the problem.

A code of infant formula marketing practices emerged from the conference that many members of the industry saw as unnecessarily crippling, but least damaging to Nestlé and its major share of market. Nestlé reorganized itself, ostensibly to face the challenges of changing late-century markets.

While the boycott seemed relatively ineffectual financially, it branded Nestlé as part of what activists of the day saw as a big-business global collusion to abuse helpless people in order to make higher profits. A venerable company's reputation had been damaged. Nestlé had, early on, delivered an inconsistent corporate response. It had deployed overly conservative tactics. It had sought technical legal redress in a matter where the only judgment of importance would be made in the court of public opinion. Its claims of a good record in nutrition-related advertising, education and research had a skeptical reception. Cultural differences got in the way, as when Swiss managers could not understand why their American counterparts could not control the media better.

Now, nearly 20 years after the publication of *The Baby Killers*, the infant formula debate continues and attitudes toward Nestlé and the role it played linger. However, the topic has left the front pages for the most part.

■ Shell/Brent Spar

Doing proper research and conforming to the law don't guarantee that a corporate decision will go down well, especially if there are environmental implications. Shell/UK learned that lesson when the company decided to dump a redundant oil storage platform in the North Sea in 1993. All requisite technical and environmental research had been done. British and international law had been followed. But Shell was not mindful of geography that gave neighboring countries a stake in the decision, and certainly the company was not sensitive either to popular sentiment or to the power of Greenpeace, the international environmental protest group that would eventually become the winning David to Shell's Goliath.

Shell was still reeling from damaged reputation and lost business, even after an admission from Greenpeace that it had not told the truth when it published certain "facts" about Brent Spar which sparked an international public and political outcry.

After 20 years of operation, Shell's Brent Spar oil rig in the North Sea was to be decommissioned in 1993 and dumped at sea. Multi-million-dollar research on the science of deep-sea dumping had been conducted and the plan met requirements of international law.

Then, Greenpeace issued a report on the dangers of sea dumping, and, despite the fact that the British Energy Ministry had approved the plan, Greenpeace activists occupied the rig and began a sophisticated communications campaign from there.

■ Boycott

Greenpeace also triggered antagonism to Shell in Germany, which considered the North Sea a "German Sea". A powerful boycott against Shell gas stations started in that country, and some stations were fire-bombed. Shell evicted Greenpeace from the rig, only to have it retaken. UK Prime Minister John Major defended Shell in Parliament, but Chancellor Helmut Kohl, under severe pressure from Germany's "greens", asked Major to withdraw the dumping permit.

International conferences, including the Oslo–Paris Convention of North Sea Nations and the European Parliament, took up the issue. The bifurcated history of European borders gave voice to Iceland, Norway, Sweden, Denmark, the Netherlands and Belgium, which, in addition to Britain and Germany, felt some ownership of the North Sea. Shell had neither consulted them nor taken into account the ferocity of animal welfare concerns among their citizenry, quite the equal to Germany's and the UK.

Three years after decommissioning Brent Spar, Shell abandoned the deep-sea dumping plan but the fallout was ultimately much more damaging to Shell than just the rig disposal about-face. Consumers, shareholders and the media across the globe were exposed to the long fight and lost faith in the venerable company. The consumer boycott in Germany cost Shell 30 per cent of its sales there and sales even plummeted at gas stations in Shell's home country of the Netherlands. Intracompany warfare ensued between Shell/UK and Shell/Germany.

"Eco-terrorism" as a strategy and "shock news" as a tactic had been tested and validated on the battlefield, as for example when a helicopter piloted by a woman tried to land Greenpeace protesters on the rig's deck and Shell used high-power water cannon to fend it off under the glare of bright lights focused on the scene for the benefit of the TV cameras. Pictures were beamed by satellite around the world and Greenpeace emerged eminently victorious.

■ Photo opportunities

"The Brent Spar shows that high profile cases, properly framed and easily explained, can ignite widespread public interest, especially if the news media get plenty of good photo opportunities," said the *Wall Street Journal/Europe*. The *Financial Times* advised that "Brent Spar means that businesses must include public opinion in environmental plans." A former Greenpeace board member commented, "Greenpeace now has a fleet of ships running around the oceans looking for something to do." A Greenpeace spokesperson promised, "The battle continues. Brent Spar is only one example. Four hundred other rigs are likely to be dumped into the North Sea."

■ The sweatshop scandal

Child labor had been used in developing countries for decades to manufacture products for American consumption, and the issue had surfaced now and then, in attacks on corporations by labor and human rights activists. Rather than read those attacks as warnings of a potential, reputation-damaging crisis, most American business was largely unconcerned, protected by industry lobbyists and public inertia.

When publicity-driven attacks targeted cultural and commercial icons in 1996, accusations of sweatshop operations against Wal-Mart and Nike made page one and network newscasts. The faces on the issue were now those of Kathie Lee Gifford, the American television talk show celebrity with a successful line of clothing at Wal-Mart stores, and Michael Jordan, the Chicago Bulls basketball hero who lent his name to Nike's Air Jordans. Other retailers and manufacturers soon were swept up in the crisis – Liz Claiborne, J.C. Penney, Talbot's, Kmart. Congress held hearings at which media-savvy activists testified; the US Labor Department and the White House were interested, too.

The issue is another example of the power of pressure groups with the media and, in particular, one battle in a long war being fought by organized labor.

Corporate response changed day by day, company to company – even though there had been plenty of warning to prepare issue management plans.

■ Complex problem

Child labor in the manufacture of name-label clothes was a complex problem. Opponents said that working children were deprived of education and innocent childhood, they took jobs adults might otherwise have, and American manufacturers were depriving higher-paid American workers of jobs. On the other hand, some economists and governments of developing nations contended that if the children were not working on American products, they would not be in school but rather working for lower wages making goods for domestic consumption; families in poverty would be deprived of the children's meager wages; and the issue was a cover for American labor protectionism. Pulling out American contracts would not resolve problems of economic standards, education and social reform, many said. Nonetheless, after she was personally attacked by a labor activist testifying before Congress, Kathie Lee Gifford wept on her syndicated television show at the suggestion she would sanction unfit conditions for child workers in order to turn a profit. Then, both she and her partner, Wal-Mart, complained the attack was unfair and they were being picked on because the clothing line was successful, making them victims of pot shots.

Though the initial charge had to do with children in a plant in Honduras, it later included workers in a New York sweatshop. Kathy Lee's sports commentator husband, Frank, visited the New York shop and gave envelopes containing $300 each, in cash, to a dozen workers after the *New York Daily News* reported that they were getting less than the minimum wage and had not been paid for months. Statements from Wal-Mart were bland, corporate, unsympathetic. The Giffords hired public relations counsel Howard J. Rubenstein Associates. They later blamed labor groups for bringing attention to the issue and the media for promoting it.

Wal-Mart announced upgraded inspections of foreign plants through an independent monitoring company and Gifford promised to hire her own outside auditor.

The response of Nike and Michael Jordan to similar attacks, by the Made in the USA Foundation, took a different tone and tactic. From the start, Jordan referred questions about the sneakers and their manufacture to Nike. The company pointed to product labels to show manufacturing was in Taiwan, not Indonesia as charged, and gave out data on its wages – twice the minimum in most of the countries where it operated. It also showed the code of conduct all its production subcontractors must sign, covering wages, overtime, safety and other standards.

■ Attack challenged

An attack was made on Kmart and actress Jaclyn Smith, whose clothing collection the store chain carries. Claims that the clothes were made by abused, low-paid teenagers in a Honduras factory were challenged by the company and the Honduran Embassy in Washington.

Many other apparel companies took another look at their policies and controls over suppliers. A very few had anticipated the potential disaster years earlier, for example Levi Strauss & Co., with its strict labor initiatives, and assessments of human rights conditions and political stability in countries where it does business. Philips Van Heusen had created a code for contractors and had been conducting surprise inspections.

The American public, however, had become sensitized. Polling cited by the Institute for Policy Studies in Washington showed that 84 per cent of US consumers said they would pay more for products manufactured overseas if they could be sure the goods were made in decent working conditions.

A newsmaking children's letter-writing crusade to companies such as Guess, Inc., manufacturers of jeans, and The Walt Disney Co., as well as to members of the US Congress, was triggered by electronic mail messages, magazine articles and television programs on child labor. Manufacturers, while denying the allegations, also contended that unions and labor activists had stirred up students, from grade school through college, to garner public support for unionizing efforts and campaigns to protect American workers.

Support has been growing in the US and other countries for an international "made without child labor" label.

Early in 1997, major sporting goods manufacturers and child advocacy groups joined in a plan to eliminate the employment of children to stitch soccer balls in Pakistan, which produces 75 per cent of the world's hand-stitched soccer balls. The plan focused on a $1 million fund to pay for independent monitors to inspect ball-making operations and a manufacturers' pledge not to sell balls made by children.

Progressing from corporate indolence to media sensation, the foreign child labor issue had triggered action and a change in public values. The cost to corporate reputations has yet to be measured.

■ StarKist "Tunagate"

Even the most vigilant company cannot know when a special-interest group or a news organization will unpredictably pay attention to its activities. The repercussions can stretch across the globe. So it pays to be ready to move quickly, to respond and stem damage, as did StarKist, the US-based tuna packing and marketing company, when it became the target of a boycott by environmentalists battling the entrapment of dolphin in tuna nets.

A member of Greenpeace had stowed away on a tuna boat to shoot videotape and he was able to capture action showing tuna fishing at its worst. His tape received broad media coverage as the issue was heating up. The tuna industry did a dive, as a consumer boycott went into action.

This case is a lesson in how companies can heal relationships with adversarial activist groups and launch market recovery campaigns that build brand share.

With the active intervention of Dr. Anthony J. O'Reilly, the CEO of its parent company, H.J. Heinz, StarKist established the industry's first dolphin-safe policy guaranteeing that they would in the future purchase tuna for packing only from ships that used nets that did not trap dolphin along with the tuna. They sought and won the support of strong and sophisticated environmental groups – including Greenpeace – that would get the word out not only to their constituencies but to consumers in general. Turning the tables on the issue, StarKist and its PR agency, Edelman Worldwide, focused consumer attention on dolphin safety, using both publicity techniques and paid advertising to create and sustain momentum for the StarKist dolphin-free policy.

■ Dolphin safety

The multi-level communications campaign started with research about journalists' attitudes, environmental groups and potential allies. Consumer studies were conducted, showing that values had shifted from price to dolphin safety. And dolphin-free product labels were tested in focus groups.

StarKist and Edelman saw that a worldwide dolphin safety program was clearly mandated, along with government oversight of fishing boats to verify compliance. They also recognized that environmentalists and American congressional leaders would have to confirm and applaud the action to make consumers believe and appreciate it. Among the organizations that lent their name and support to the StarKist campaign were Greenpeace and its formidable globe-spanning reputation, the United States Humane Society and Earth Island, all of which sent representatives to StarKist's well-attended press conference in Washington, DC, announcing the dolphin-free policy.

Coverage on network and local television, in news magazines, local newspapers and wire services was extensive. Earth Day, just a week later, offered another opportunity to create visibility. Celebrities, including actors Tom Cruise and Ted Danson, praised StarKist at rallies in Los Angeles and Washington.

Activists lifted the boycott against StarKist, and some even placed advertising asking consumers to press other tuna companies to adopt the StarKist standard.

■ The mad cow disease feeding frenzy

Mishandled communications by a government can create a global crisis. That was the case in 1996, when the British government did not anticipate the panic that would be created domestically and internationally by its lackadaisical treatment of a scientific study suggesting a possible link between a serious disease in cows and a similar one in humans.

In what came to be known widely as the "mad cow" problem, Britain's Ministry of Agriculture, Fisheries and Food released a report citing strong evidence that there was a connection between Bovine Spongiform Encephalopathy [BSE], a brain disease, and the human version, Creutzfeld-Jacob Disease, a deadly illness which also affects the brain. The announcement of a "very worrying" link came after ten years of government denial that BSE posed any health risk to human beings, an embarrassing reversal. Making matters worse, the government did not put the new information in perspective for the general public.

There was no word that more study was necessary, or that the risk was minimal because bovine organs and spinal material, affected by the disease, are not allowed in foods, or that added measures had been in place for years to prevent the disease's spread.

Hungry for a sensational story, the media focused on the fact that some scientists had conjectured that every cow in the country – 11 million animals – might have to be put to death and that 500,000 people could die of the disease.

■ Commission astonished

Restaurants closed. Schools no longer served beef. France, Belgium, the Netherlands, Portugal and Sweden joined the United States in keeping English beef out – the US having taken that stand seven years earlier. The UK Meat and Livestock Commission was astonished it had received no prior warning of the study, and it hired Lowe Bell Communications to help handle the crisis. Others in private industry did their best to allay consumer fears. For example, McDonald's put out the word that its hamburgers were made of top-quality prime beef, containing no risk-carrying carcasses.

Despite the facts that there continued to be no proof that mad cow disease can go from cattle to humans, and that there was no evidence of the variant form of Creutzfeld-Jakob disease in the US, the American beef industry moved swiftly and dramatically. The National Cattleman's Beef Association joined with the American Sheep Industry Association, because sheep carry a similar disease and sheep offal is used to feed cows. The two groups linked up with the National Milk Producers Federation, the American Veterinary Medical Association, the American Association of Bovine Practitioners and the American Association of Veterinary Medical Colleges, in a collaboration to ensure that feed for cows did not include protein derived from cows and sheep. The coalition supported US Food and Drug Administration (FDA) regulations on this prohibition and pressed for the Department of Agriculture to step up its oversight activities and conduct research and education programs. Reassuringly, the group said a ten-year government study of BSE had found no evidence of the illness in American cattle and the new actions were preventive.

Subsequently, the FDA proposed a ban that would start in 1997 of the use of any tissue from ruminant animals, such as cattle, sheep and goats, in making animal feed.

On balance, the efforts to respond to the crisis in Britain were too little, too late; substantial harm had been done to the credibility of the government and the beef industry.

■ Slow start for Audi on involuntary acceleration

Aggressive, open communications policies often rise from the ashes of a badly handled crisis. The television and print press had jumped all over Audi in 1986, with stories accusing the company of making cars that accelerated unintentionally, taking off at full throttle on their own, even if the driver stood on the brake.

Though automotive writers, who understood car engineering, did not believe the charges and debunked the criticism, plenty of willing drivers wanted to be interviewed on television and in consumer media, to blame their accidents on their Audis.

The company's response: blame the customer, give complicated engineering explanations centered on driver error, withhold information altogether. Unattributed suggestions pointed the finger at rival automakers for fanning the flames.

Audi's opponents, however, used publicity techniques to link every known problem involving Audi to unintended acceleration.

The results were predictable, led by a dramatic plunge in sales. Major investigations were launched in the US, Canada and Japan. Right after a damaging *60 Minutes* broadcast in 1986, a national telephone poll in the US showed that more than 90 per cent of the population believed something was wrong with the Audi and more than 80 per cent thought Audi was deliberately covering up by blaming the problem on drivers. Complaints multiplied and more than 100 law suits were filed.

■ Advocacy advertising

Reflecting internal dissension about the course to follow, a series of Audi executives seemed unable to take effective counteraction until early 1988, when the fourth chief executive in 16 months, Richard Mugg, decided to fight back. He activated advocacy advertising and media relations. A team composed of public relations, legal and technical service staffers was to investigate and cool down allegations. A "fire brigade" of public relations and legal representatives would monitor events and respond. Eight- to ten-second responses to every possible question were developed and committed to memory by all spokespersons. Every request for an interview with a senior manager was honored. A public relations firm with strong credentials in the automotive industry, Casey Communications Management, was hired to counsel and help implement the new actions.

What the automotive writers had known finally became general knowledge, as the Canadian government issued a report saying no defect existed in the cars and unintended acceleration was, indeed, the result of driver error. A similar conclusion was reached by the Japanese government, and the US government issued a report saying the problem occurred when "the operator steps on the gas when he thinks he's on the brake." Simple.

The Audi Information Network, a public relations tactic, was activated to spread the news of the findings, and the media began more positive reporting. Opponents were refuted in the courts. By mid-1990, four consecutive quarters of sales gains were recorded. The new Audi open-door policy toward the media was entrenched.

This was an interesting example of a crisis created by "exposé", with a good "recovery" program.

■ Pepsi syringe scare

When corporate and product reputations are of the highest order, the buffeting of crises is diminished. That was the case with Pepsi-Cola Company when incidents of tampering with Diet Pepsi cans began being reported in June 1993. A high degree of consumer trust combined with decisive company action to end, within a week, what could have been a global disaster involving a high-volume, high-visibility product.

Initially, a Seattle television station reported someone had discovered a hypodermic syringe in a can of Diet Pepsi. Subsequent, similar reports led to a Food and Drug Administration [FDA] regional advisory that consumers empty the contents of their Diet Pepsi cans into a glass before drinking. The events made national news and within hours, other regions of the country were reporting more incidents. The traditionally high sales volume during the July 4th Independence Day holiday was threatened.

Fortunately, crisis management and response guidelines had been in place at Pepsi, and periodically tested and revised, for ten years. Pepsi officials knew that effective communication is the key to crisis resolution and they went into action on Day One of the syringe scare. The Seattle bottler initiated an investigation and responded readily to the media and the public. A crisis team worked to reassure consumers of Pepsi product safety and leveraged trust in the 95-year-old Pepsi trademark. The driving theme was that a planned tampering involving syringes could not logically take place in current product manufacturing practices and a recall would not solve the problem. The company communicated early and often with media and all audiences, and worked with the FDA to investigate how syringes could have found their way into Pepsi cans. Audiences included media, regulatory officials, bottlers, shareholders, employees and customers such as retail stores, restaurants and Pepsi sales outlets.

At first, the agenda was to understand the problem, rule out sabotage, provide on-site interviews in Seattle and media access to the high-tech plant there, and issue company press releases assuring the public that Pepsi would discover the answer.

■ Vicious cycle

The FDA quickly found a "vicious cycle of media reports begetting copycat complaints." Pepsi's crisis team created video news releases, press releases, consumer talking points, bottler advisories, employee bulletins, trade letters, graphics and interview opportunities, particularly aimed at reaching audiences that could help Pepsi and the FDA bring the scare to an end. Recognizing that television would reach the widest audiences quickly, Pepsi and media consultant Robert Chang produced compelling video footage, showing the speed and safety of the manufacturing process and the illogicality of the complaints simultaneously occurring in different locations.

Pepsi CEO Craig Wetherup appeared on major network news programs to reassure viewers the tampering could not be happening in Pepsi plants. Some 70 media and consumer specialists, aided by volunteers, staffed phones. Advisories were faxed twice daily to 400 bottling plants and additional Pepsi staff counseled bottlers and field personnel on local issues. FDA national and local officials were crisis counselors to the company and focused on finding the cause of the tampering claims, while Pepsi concentrated on demonstrating that its package and process were tamper-proof.

Having suffered $25 million in lost sales, Pepsi ultimately bounced back and ended its summer season with record sales. Even more important, the company documented consumer confidence. At the peak of the crisis, attitude and awareness surveys showed 94 per cent of consumers believed Pepsi was handling it responsibly; 75 per cent said they felt better about Pepsi products because of the way the company had responded. The cooperation of the FDA and among bottlers and customers in resisting demand for a national recall of Pepsi products was unprecedented. In editorials, the news media questioned their role in escalating consumer and business fear of unsubstantiated product tampering. Even the US House of Representatives took note, with an entry in the Congressional Record praising Pepsi for quick and decisive action to end the national scare.

■ The first Internet-age crisis – Pentium chip

An industry-wide crisis of credibility threatened when a single prominent manufacturer dug in its heels about a product malfunction and the news went out on the Internet. The protagonists were no less than the computer industry and Intel with its new, vaunted Pentium chip, in what *Fortune* magazine called "a brouhaha that always was more about PR than actual product problems." The handling of this crisis was an unusual PR fumble for Intel, which was voted third most admired company in the USA in *Fortune* magazine's 1997 ranking.

In mid-1994, a mathematics professor found computing problems occurred with his Pentium-equipped computer. Intel told him he was one of some 2 million Pentium users who had reported the same "obscure" problem, a response the professor and his friends posted on the Internet, reaching 20 to 30 million people globally. The problem initiated use of the Internet as a crisis-publicity tool, in advance of media coverage. Intel told customers who requested a replacement chip that they had to prove they needed one. Massive advertising for the Pentium chip stayed on track. The company had calculated that the problem would affect a spreadsheet user once every 27,000 years, and this did not justify a consumer alert or product recall.

■ IBM stops shipments

But by the end of the year, IBM, concerned for its customers, announced it had decided to stop shipments of its high-powered PCs equipped with the flawed Pentium chip and said that Intel had severely underestimated the chip's potential for error. That decision was front-page news. Some observers cynically said this was an IBM PR offensive, not justified by the mere 5 per cent of its computers carrying Pentium chips but rather boosting IBM's future competition with Intel in the chip business. Intel executives were mostly unresponsive to media calls. One apologist said the company was not accustomed to dealing with end-users.

Pentium's largest client, Dell Computer, made no public announcement but dealt directly with Intel and customers to remedy the problem. Dell knew affected customers would be those doing sophisticated calculations and statistics.

With unhappy computer users growing in number and its lesson brutally learned, Intel in late December said it would replace the flawed Pentium chip for anyone who wanted one, without questions asked. In full-page newspaper ads, the company apologized for its bland handling of consumer complaints. But a great deal of damage had already been done, not just to Intel's reputation but to the credibility of the entire computer industry. Consultants, computer columnists and business reporters were advising companies and individuals to put off buying Pentium-equipped computers until corrected chips became available. It was expected that, henceforth, new computer technology would be more thoroughly tested and therefore introduced more slowly. The heart of the damage had been preventable, through candor, generous handling of consumer complaints and quick response to the media.

■ Takeovers and mergers

It is not hard to identify companies that are ripe for acquisition. Indeed, the financial writers in the business press periodically publish lists of such companies in different fields. There are any number of reasons why a company should be included: it might have large assets but low earnings. It might be too small to compete with its larger rivals. It might have an alternative product pipeline which the predator company wants or feels it can develop more successfully. The geographical strength of the target company may prove a good fit. There are many more reasons.

Likely target companies can and should be aware of the likelihood of a bid and should plan accordingly. Nonetheless, the announcement of a takeover bid often comes as a surprise, with the target company ill-prepared to repel the advances.

Even if the eventual acquisition of the company is a foregone conclusion, a strong defense can influence the price that is paid and even the ultimate merger partner.

Today, it is increasingly the case that non-financial considerations can play a major role in making or breaking a political merger, a fertile field in which the public relations practitioner can play a key role. Anti-trust and defense factors often weigh heavily in the matter.

And then, of course, there is chauvinism. A recent example played itself out in France, the country of Chauvin, a Napoleonic veteran 200 years ago.

■ France/Thomson

No one had predicted the strength of popular negative feeling in France, about selling off a state-owned electronics company, a division of which would have ended up in South Korean hands.

As part of a privatization plan and an effort to reduce its military-industrial complex, France had decided in 1996 to sell Thomson S.A. to Lagardere Group, a French company mostly interested in the military component of Thomson. Lagardere planned to spin off the consumer division of Thomson to Daewoo Electronics Company of South Korea.

Thomson was heavily indebted and had already eaten up substantial French government resources. It was not lean enough to compete with American companies. Still, the French people were prouder of it and more attached to it than government leaders had anticipated. A furious protest to the proposed sale ensued, ultimately halting it.

The *New York Times* captured the problem in its reporting: "...The terms of the sale to Lagardere had set off a storm of protest by the opposition Socialist Party and labor unions, who denounced the idea of giving away part of the national patrimony in the name of market efficiency – and to foreigners, to boot...

"But the main thing against it was the national mood in France, where 'globalization' and 'market efficiency' are becoming dirty words as government austerity policies aimed at making France more fit for international competition have helped keep unemployment at 12.6 per cent of the labor force."

■ Insult

Anti-Asian sentiment was an undercurrent, topped by the added insult that the sales were set for the token price of one franc each.

Officially, the government ended the episode by saying final approval of the sale had been withheld out of concern about transferring advanced technology to a foreign country. The promise of substantial infusion of funds and job creation by both Lagardere and Daewoo had not reversed popular sentiment. It is probable that both acted too little and too late to explain the benefits of the plan.

Once the sale cancellation was made public, the French government announced intentions to privatize Thomson in two stages, starting with the defense business, the multimedia one later.

Characterizing the episode as symptomatic of a failing government, *The Economist* concluded: "France's leaders have a straightforward choice: to encourage the largely healthy revolution that is already beginning to refashion French commerce, or to resist it – and watch it happen anyway."

■ British Airways world's biggest offer

It is not sufficient to prepare for and manage a crisis when it hits. Forward planning requires that there be a "recovery" plan in place to rebuild the business that might have been badly damaged by a catastrophe. It does not matter whether the cause was human error, engineering failure or "act of God" as the insurance companies categorize events over which you have no control.

Companies that operate globally feel the impact whenever there are tumultuous world events.

The repercussions are especially dramatic for the travel and tourism industry, as British Airways and other airlines learned in 1986, immediately following the bombing of Libya and the Chernobyl reactor explosion. Four years later, the passengers, crew and ground staff of a British Airways [BA] flight landing in Kuwait were detained as "guests" of the Iraqi government, during the Gulf War. A recession was already under way and air travel had been substantially reduced. News of the Kuwait incident appeared on television and in newspapers, precipitating further losses.

Early on in the Gulf war British Airways recognized that there was little they could do to encourage air travel while hostilities continued. However, they did create a "recovery" task force which spent three months planning a high profile campaign to "jump start" air travel once again after the war ended. There was a big gap to make up because business had dropped by 30 per cent. The model for action already existed. It had been created in response to the 1986 losses. Then, the "Go for it America" campaign had sent 5,000 lucky travelers on cost-free sprees from the USA to Great Britain. This earlier success prompted BA to create "The World's Biggest Offer" in 1990, a $100 million promotion "to get the world flying again".

■ Every seat free

Working again with Edelman Public Relations Worldwide, BA announced that on April 23, every seat in its system would be free. People holding tickets would fly free and other seats would be raffled through a coupon entry, for a total of 50,000 free seats. As in the earlier program, the new campaign would include special offers from hotels, car rental companies, restaurants, theaters and stores.

The global campaign, masterminded in London, required secrecy until launch day and was coordinated among BA's in-house PR managers and 42 consultancies. The tactics had to be replicated throughout the world and all press materials were localized and translated.

Announcement press conferences around the globe were held simultaneously. The entry and selection process was then monitored for anecdotes with publicity potential.

On April 23, dubbed "Up and Away Day", bobbies, bag pipers and other costumed characters were in 62 airports in BA gateway cities, and 435 previously pitched reporters, photographers and broadcast crews from 60 countries covered the winners' trips to London. Photo opportunities were set up with the British Prime Minister and Transport Minister.

The complex effort yielded major print and television coverage, including all national TV networks in the US. Worldwide, some 500 million people read about the campaign and 200 million saw it on television. There had been a grand total of 5.7 million entries and BA was able to add millions of qualified names with travel preferences to its database. Recovery from the travel slump was complete within 120 days. Every major travel market in the world was stimulated.

CHAPTER 10

Public Affairs

It is fashionable nowadays among many people in communications to describe their work broadly as Public Affairs, implying that public relations is a branch of that umbrella activity, rather than the opposite. I will not debate here the appropriate terminology because so many words have been spoken or written on that subject elsewhere. Suffice to say that for our purposes we will take the term "public affairs" to mean that part of the communications activity that is directed toward government representatives at local, national and supra-national level. These representatives may be elected legislators or the civil servants whose translation of laws into a host of regulations can often have more impact than the laws themselves.

In this chapter, we will focus our attention primarily on the USA, partly because there the activity is well regulated and documented, and because the US market is so important for all organizations operating globally. In addition, US government agencies such as the Food and Drug Administration (FDA) exert an influence well beyond the borders of the USA.

Public Affairs is sometimes loosely referred to as Lobbying, but we should be more precise. While many activities covered by a public affairs executive can be described as lobbying with a small "l", Lobbying with a capital "L" has traditionally had a particular and regulated meaning in the USA and in Great Britain.

"A Lobbyist" deals directly with lawmakers, regulators and their various committees. The very word 'lobbyist' arises because the practitioner hangs around the lobbies of Congress and the Senate, or the Houses of Parliament in Britain, hoping to waylay lawmakers as they move to and from their chambers.

But the distinctions are becoming blurred.

■ US lobbying

The majority of mainstream public relations firms in the USA do not undertake lobbying as described above. It is the province of law firms, individuals and highly specialized companies.

Many individuals who run the representative offices of companies close to the centers of government are informally or formally registered as lobbyists under the appropriate local code.

But, in the USA, the code was substantially tightened when Congress passed the Lobbying Disclosure Act (LDA), which took effect in January 1997, and reformed laws that had been in effect since 1946. It eliminated the distinction between the small "l" and capital "L" lobbyist in the USA, as far as the letter of the law is concerned, although in PR circles the distinction remains as a way to distinguish between the activities of individuals and firms practicing the different kinds of public affairs.

The LDA said a company's public relations agency rather than the company itself might qualify as lobbyists and be required to register with Congress and the Justice Department. "Many public relations activities that no one would previously have dreamed of calling 'lobbying' now fall under that category," warned attorney Thomas P. Steindler of McDermott, Will & Energy (Washington, DC), an expert on the new requirements. "As always in law, ignorance is no excuse, and noncompliance can be costly, with civil penalties amounting to as much as $50,000," he said after the Act's passage.

The new rules also say that client companies or their agencies cannot pick up a restaurant tab when they're with members of the House of Representatives or their staff members.

On the Senate side, the new rules allow you to pay for meals of Senators or their staffers, if the meals cost less than $50 (with a $100 annual limit). "I foresee a rise in the number of chats taking place at hot-dog stands," joked Steindler, referring to the fact that meals valued at less than $10 do not count toward the $100 annual limit.

As newly defined in the LDA, a "lobbyist" is any individual who is paid by a third party to make more than one "lobbying contact". A lobbying contact is an oral or written communication to a vast range of specific individuals (or specific job titles) in the Executive and Legislative branches of the Federal Government. These are "covered" individuals. Which brings us to the question of what constitutes "lobbying activities"? Lobbying activities are lobbying contacts and efforts in support of such contacts, including preparation and planning activities, research and other background work that is intended at the time it is performed for use in contacts, and coordination with the lobbying activities of others.

For the first time, the definition of "lobbying activities" covers research and other background work, as long as it is prepared for a lobbying purpose. Therefore, if you or your PR agency prepare an issue brief for a member of congress or staffer, or you have an informal meeting for that purpose, it would be treated as a lobbying activity. So, you are required to register. There's a loophole: "Under the new law, not just your actions but your intentions matter: preparation of a study for some purpose other than lobbying would not be considered a lobbying activity – even if the study were later to be used in the course of lobbying activities," said Steindler.

What about the definition of "lobbying contact"? It refers to any oral or written communication to a covered official that is made on behalf of a client and relates to formulation/adoption of Federal legislation or a Federal rule, regulation, Executive order, or any other program/policy/position of the US Government; administration/ execution of a Federal program or policy; nomination or confirmation for a position subject to confirmation by the Senate.

Exemptions to the definition of lobbying contact include communications made in a speech, article, publication, or other material distributed to the public through radio, television or other medium of mass communication; testimony presented to a committee or task force of Congress; and comments filed in the course of a public proceeding or in response to a Federal Register notice.

■ Aides included

One of the most dramatic changes from the 1946 law relates to the definition of a "covered official." These are members of Congress, and, for the first time, congressional staffers. The 1946 law covered only members, not their aides.

"Inclusion of congressional staffers is a tip-off to the intent of those who drafted the new legislation," said Tom Steindler. "They know that 90 per cent of lobbying gets done at the staff level, and they wanted to make sure that the real movers and shakers were covered by the law."

The new LDA is cross-referenced with reporting requirements under the Foreign Agents Registration Act (FARA), which covers work done for foreign entities, foreign governments and/or foreign political parties.

Anyone required to register under the LDA as or on behalf of a foreign commercial entity is exempt from registering under FARA. And anyone required to file under FARA as or on behalf of a foreign government and/or foreign political party is exempt from registering under the LDA.

It is vital for non-US PR executives to understand FARA. Many foreign organizations prefer not to believe that it exists. It is dangerous to take this view. Penalties for willful violation can be a fine of up to $10,000 or imprisonment for up to five years.

Virtually all representations of foreign governments and foreign political parties require registration under FARA, even if the representation does not involve traditional lobbying and is confined to public relations, investment and trade promotion, tourism promotion, or the like.

There is a gray area in which work for a foreign corporation can involve the political or public interests of a foreign country. Examples include promotion of the sale in the US of so-called "political" products, which have included Cuban sugar, coffee from certain South American countries, and textiles from Japan.

If in doubt, the rule is register or seek advice from legal counsel.

■ FARA

FARA is strict in its requirements. Agencies must file before beginning registrable work for a client and in any event within ten days of signing a contract. And the contract itself, along with the financial terms, has to be submitted and immediately becomes open to public view. Naive governments are sometimes shocked when they hear that not only their PR strategies and tactics are available to all, including their political opponents at home, but the cost as well. The lesson is to be prudent in the detailed action program that is disclosed in the written contract.

Disclosure is not a one-time event. FARA calls for a report of all activities and payments every six months. The reports require a detailed, itemized statement for every news release issued, every meeting held and more besides.

Not only must meticulous reports be prepared and submitted within 48 hours of a news release but all written materials must be labeled with a statement declaring that the PR firm is registered at a specific federal court. Labels all basically must follow the wording of the example shown below, used by my own firm in its work for the

Government of Egypt. *"This material is prepared, edited, issued or circulated by Edelman Public Relations Worldwide, 1500 Broadway, New York, NY 10036, which is registered with the Department of Justice, Washington, DC, under the Foreign Agents Registration Act as an agent of The Egypt Ministry of Foreign Affairs. This material is filed with the Department of Justice where the required registration statement is available for public inspection. Registration does not indicate approval of the contents of the material by the United States Government."* Additionally, a FARA label or its equivalent must appear at the beginning of any motion picture film or videotape distributed on behalf of a registered client.

Few countries have regulations as stringent as the USA but all have their own rules and customs. It behooves the international PR practitioner to familiarize himself with those that apply in all markets of importance to his organization.

Obviously relationships with government are more important for some companies than others. Defense contractors, oil and mining companies, utilities and others that rely on their ability to use natural – and national – resources, along with other heavily regulated organizations such as airlines, and radio and television companies, are all dependent on government decisions that can deliver or cost huge amounts of money to the income statements.

■ Trade associations and public affairs

Because many of the issues arising at the governmental level affect all companies in a particular industry, trade associations, described more fully earlier as a PR specialty, are the mechanism by which many companies handle a large number of their public affairs issues. In Washington today, no fewer than 1,830 trade associations have their headquarters or a satellite office engaged in government relations. In Brussels, headquarters of the supra-national European Commission, there are offices with "lobbyists" representing 40 different branches of agriculture in France alone.

And for many companies, governments are the largest buyers of their products or services.

There is not a single organization that does not have some reason to think about and act on a public affairs policy. From the day doors are opened for business – and even before – there are numerous contacts with various forms of government. Permission to locate the business at your selected site is probably the first contact, followed by dealing with local ordinances, and labor practice laws, and paying local and federal taxes. All these issues affect General Motors as well as the sole proprietor of a PR counseling practice that operates from a home office. Although Public Affairs is largely practiced at the local level, every public relations practitioner aspiring to an international career needs an understanding of the different government structures in important markets, as well as of the customary ways of dealing with officials in a variety of countries.

■ Tenneco Report

An excellent example of a public affairs campaign that achieved total success in a notoriously difficult market – Japan – was the "Tenneco Report", winner of the overall prize in the 1997 Golden World Awards of the IPRA.

Tenneco Automotive, a major US auto-parts manufacturer, had made little progress over 20 years in selling its shock absorbers in Japan. In 1994, it had only a 3.5 per cent share of shock-absorber sales in the after-market there. After hiring Inoue Public Relations to help turn the situation around, extensive research was conducted, which disclosed that:

- Japanese legislation over 40 years had established standards for car safety, maintenance and the inspection system that protected the domestic after-market, with no room for imported parts.
- Domestically manufactured auto parts were labeled "genuine OE (original equipment) parts" but imported parts were handicapped by being labeled "non-OE parts".
- Most certified auto-repair shops were controlled by top Japanese auto makers, who had relationships with domestic parts manufacturers.
- Operators of repair shops were conservative by nature, resisting change.
- Imported parts were made more expensive by Japan's complex distribution system.

The research findings were compiled in "The Tenneco Report", which would become pivotal throughout the campaign.

Tenneco's objectives were to secure deregulation of the Japanese auto-parts after-market, find new business partners for distribution of Tenneco products, and create new demand by re-educating Japanese car owners regarding purchase of shock absorbers.

Among the critical audiences to reach were key ministries in the Japanese government, industry groups such as the Japan Auto Parts Industry Association, car shops, prospective new distribution channels such as gas stations, and industry experts. Media targets were newspapers, news agencies, business and trade press, TV stations and the foreign press.

The Tenneco Report was initially delivered to the US Department of Commerce and the US Trade Representative office; then it went to the White House. In Japan, it was given to high-ranking officials in the Ministry of Trade and Industry (MITI) and Ministry of Transport (MOT), and the American Embassy, with unofficial briefings for the ministries.

On October 1, 1994, President Clinton declared US intentions to apply trade sanctions to Japan as a result of the auto-parts after-market situation.

Behind-the-scenes discussions with both governments continued, focused on the Tenneco Report. Off-the-record briefings were conducted for major Japanese newspapers and TV stations, which had previously depended on the Japanese government for their information.

Negotiations between the US Trade Representative and the Japanese Government stalled just before a June 28, 1995, deadline, and the US threatened to enforce sanctions. Media coverage of the negotiations, informed by the Tenneco briefings, had a major impact on public opinion, which put pressure on the Japanese government to settle.

With deregulation under way, Tenneco successfully negotiated distribution partnerships with Toyota Motors, Autobacs, an auto-parts 380-store chain, and

Japan Energy, one of the country's major oil companies with 6,400 "JOMO" gas stations.

A press conference to launch the sale of Tenneco shock absorbers was held at a JOMO gas station, a "first" in Japan. It was covered by more than 100 Japanese and foreign journalists.

Armed with an information update, Tenneco Inc. Chairman and CEO Dana Mead met with high-ranking Japanese officials to get their support for further opening of the auto-parts after-market.

Throughout the campaign, extensive and quality coverage was generated as a result of one-on-one interviews and mailings of press releases. *Nihon Keizai Shimbun*, equivalent to the *Financial Times* or the *Wall Street Journal*, published a special report after a settlement was reached in Geneva between Japan and the US; it revealed the existence of the Tenneco Report and its influence on the talks.

The most important results were:

- fast action by the Japanese Ministry of Transport to exclude shock absorbers from the list of auto parts requiring inspection, which made possible the sale of the products at locations not certified as inspection stations;
- instructions sent by MITI to distributors, telling them not to discriminate against foreign-made products;
- instructions from the Ministry of Transport to auto-repair shops not to discriminate and to allow consumers to select the shock absorbers they wanted.

Sales of Tenneco shock absorbers increased more than 40 per cent in Japan from 1995 to 1996. President Clinton, in an April 1996 White House press conference marking the successful end of US–Japan auto negotiations, honored the achievements of Tenneco in Japan.

■ New genre of public affairs

With the liberalizing of world trade, the reduction of tariff barriers and the formation of regional trading groups, a more integrated international genre of public affairs is growing up.

Some individuals have special knowledge of particular institutions, such as the Commission, Parliament and Council of Ministers of the European Union; others have a deep expertise on global or multi-country institutions, such the United Nations, OECD and the World Trade Organization.

Increasingly, issues are being decided at the supra-national level that were once resolved at the national level, whether a charge of illegal "dumping" of cheap goods in a market or a dispute over access to a particular market (such as the case between Kodak and Fuji Film).

Practitioners who once were used to dealing effectively at the national level now have to enhance their understanding of what it takes to win when matters are adjudicated at the international level.

Many of the issues-resolution techniques commonly used in the USA are gradually being adopted in locally customized format in many other countries. (In fact, there is a minor industry growing up in which experts in this area devote much of their time to transferring their knowledge to institutions in other countries eager to adopt the American methods.) One such method, coalition or alliance building, has been briefly mentioned in the section on trade associations.

Coalitions and alliances play a powerful role in times of change, especially when legislation or a ruling by a government department has a major impact – for good or ill – on a particular group of organizations. Some examples are:

- an alliance formed by American Airlines, United Airlines and Delta Airlines to fight the proposed strategic alliance that British Airways and US Air were seeking to establish;
- an alliance established between the normally deadly rivals United Parcel Service and Fedex to prevent negative, misleading television advertising from the United States Postal Service;
- the Coalition of Long Distance Carriers (CLDC), a group of long distance telephone companies, led by AT&T, MCI and Sprint, to ensure that the major Telecom Act which was going through Congress in 1995 and 1996 was not unduly favorable to the local Bell operating companies as a result of their immense lobbying power and resources.

■ Grassroots campaigns

Health care reform ... most favored trade status for China ... telephone deregulation ... tax reform ... mining law reform ... utility deregulation ... the North American Free Trade Agreement ... These major legislative initiatives, as singular issues, could not be more different, yet they have one thing in common – they either passed or failed because of public opinion shaped by effective, well-organized grassroots lobbying campaigns. For years, these issues languished in the legislative arena. They were finally acted upon and resolved once the public weighed in.

Although grassroots activism, in a much simpler form than is common today, has a long and proud tradition in American politics, there is no doubt that it has become a very sophisticated and integral part of the American political process.

Environmental and labor groups gave life to the modern grassroots campaign. Today, however, corporations and coalitions of different organizations are embracing the practice. Indeed, any organization that intends to influence the lawmaking process needs to incorporate grassroots lobbying in its plan because it is a primary weapon in the legislative arsenal.

How does a grassroots campaign differ from public relations when it comes to influencing public policy? Whereas a public relations program generally consists of one organization getting out a message through the use of media relations activities, grassroots lobbying campaigns are marked by the organized, systematic implementation of a wide-ranging series of "political-campaign-style" activities undertaken by a large number of people. All of the communications actions are geared to ensuring a certain legislative outcome. Messages are sent directly to lawmakers as well as delivered through the news media. If one is looking for a simple definition, a grassroots campaign may be described as "any technique that provides the 'folks back home' with information designed to stimulate communications" by letters, telegrams, and meetings. (*The Lobbying Handbook*, John L. Zorack, 1990.)

The grassroots campaign is organized like a political campaign. Every campaign covers four phases: identification, education, mobilization and activation of an "interested public". The tools or vehicles used to deliver messages for the purpose of impacting legislation include personal letters, mailgrams, telephone calls, personal contacts and special events designed to attract media coverage.

Why does grassroots campaigning work? It matters to a politician what people back home think, since they control the electoral fate of the official. Former Speaker of the US House of Representatives Tip O'Neil coined the phrase that "all politics is local", and he was dead right.

Among the first highly visible and successful grassroots campaigns in America was one that was conducted by the banks and brokerage houses in 1985. These corporate entities used grassroots efforts to defeat legislation that would have required them to withhold a percentage of their customers' interest and dividends for taxation.

Edelman Worldwide is implementing two major grassroots campaigns, one for FujiFilm and the other for AT&T. The campaign for FujiFilm focuses on activating the company's US employees so that the US Trade Representative, key members of Congress and interested officials in the Clinton Administration understand how trade sanctions imposed on the Japanese government would negatively and unfairly impact thousands of American workers.

The AT&T campaign in support of competition in local telephone markets is practically identical to an American presidential campaign. A national campaign office led by a "campaign manager" directs the activities of "field coordinators" who are responsible for mobilizing public opinion. A national media relations program is complemented by local efforts. All of the communications and political actions are issue-driven and advocate a particular outcome.

Getting involved in a campaign for a cause is an exciting way to participate in the civic process and exercise your right to be heard on issues that are important to you. Also, it is rewarding to know that for each person who steps into the arena and gets involved, democracy grows healthier.

■ Environmental affairs

Environmental communications are either considered a full-fledged specialty, a part of consumer communications or integral to public affairs.

Interest in environmental issues is spread across business and consumer constituencies. Manufacturers face laws and challenges regarding plant siting, recycling and chemical disposal. Consumers take up the causes of forest preservation and keeping carcinogens out of everyday products.

The twinning of environmental communications with public affairs is because governments, at the national or local level, are decisive institutions in matters of the environment. Lawmakers can vote to implement recycling projects, for example, that will cost millions or close down plants in violation of emissions laws, and thus possibly eliminate jobs in the short term for a perceived long-term economic and social advantage. Or they can frustrate the attempts of environmentalists, represented by well-organized pressure groups, to enact protective legislation.

The field is an important one for communications professionals. A number of specialist practices experienced in and knowledgeable about environmental affairs have established themselves in several countries, including the US, the UK, Germany and France.

CHAPTER 11

Sponsorship? Philanthropy? Or Promotion?

The finest athletes who competed in the ancient Olympic Games in Greece were celebrated heroes whose company was sought by the most influential figures in the democracy at that time.

Nero and other Roman emperors two millennia ago arranged spectacular events in arenas such as the Coliseum in Rome where gladiators fought each other and wild animals as well.

The Popes in Rome and families such as the Borgias and the Medicis provided encouragement, subsidies and shelter to a host of renaissance artists such as Leonardo da Vinci, Michaelangelo and Benvenuto Cellini as a memorial to their power, wealth and good taste, and in so doing gave the world lasting treasures of inestimable value.

Emperors, kings, princes and archbishops in Europe and elsewhere maintained orchestras, theatrical troupes and composers. We must thank them for Monteverdi, Vivaldi, Bach and Mozart.

More recently, communism created its own state patronage system, in which athletes were provided sinecures in the military so that they could practice and win gold medals in world championship events and Olympiads. In the arts and entertainment, the same regimes patronized the arts through such institutions as the Bolshoi Ballet and the Moscow State Circus as a way of maintaining the prestige of the state.

Yet many of us persist in seeing the huge growth in sponsorship and event management as a recent phenomenon rather than evolution in which industry and commerce have taken over the role of patron or sponsor from the ecclesiastical hierarchy, the aristocracy or ruling totalitarian party. It is a role that has been played through the centuries by whichever group was most powerful and rich.

Sponsorship (I will use that word with a small "s" to embrace all the activities described in this chapter; a capital "S" when applied specifically to the more narrowly defined underwriting of particular events) is of vital importance to anyone aspiring to practice international public relations.

It is one of the few activities that can eliminate boundaries and borders when it is well understood and practiced with skill.

According to the international CORPerceptions research regularly conducted by ORC (Opinion Research Corporation), those companies engaged in sponsorship of major world class events such as the Olympics or the World Cup achieve higher favorable ratings than non-sponsors. It is apparent that in certain countries more kudos is given to these major sponsors than in others.

Dr. Jim Fink of ORC interprets this phenomenon thus: "People are impressed by companies that are major sponsors of worldwide events. Not only do they assume they have the money to buy the rights, but somehow they feel they have been selected for this position of honor from among their competitors. In several eastern countries where the notion of 'face' is of the highest importance, to be an Olympic sponsor ensures you the highest level of 'face'. It signals that your company has arrived at the pinnacle of its industry."

Moreover, to be a top-tier sponsor of the Olympic Games or World Cup immediately classifies your organization as global. There would be little point in paying the extremely high entrance fee for the worldwide rights (US$40 million for the most recent pair of summer/winter Games) unless you operate in all the world's markets. The names of recent top-tier sponsors of the two premier events underline this assertion.

For the World Cup in 1998, the Top-Tier Sponsors are FujiFilm, Mastercard, Mars, Canon, EDS, Hewlett Packard, Budweiser, France Telecom and LaPoste.

For the Olympics in Nagano (1998) and Sydney (2000), the prime worldwide Top IV Partner categories have been claimed by IBM, Kodak, UPS, Samsung, Coca Cola, VISA, Panasonic, Xerox, John Hancock and Sports Illustrated, as shown on the Olympics website. Also shown are sponsors of other levels who may be entitled to use the Olympic rings in their promotional materials.

But the major world championship events are not the only avenue for international companies with smaller purses – or incompatible goals – to include sponsorship as a key element in the communications strategy.

As an international public relations executive, you will be one of several people within your organization who may have a hand in selecting sponsorships. If publicity is the most important aim of the sponsorship, your opinion will carry much weight, but that is not always the case. The important thing to keep in mind as you analyze the options and make your selections for recommendation is that you must stay in control of the process. The road to selection and, after selection, management and exploitation of the sponsorship, offers many enticing detours, hairpin bends and landslides to block your progress, but few roadsigns.

The first problem you will encounter in most companies that are quite new to sponsorship is that there is a lack of understanding on the part of many senior executives as to the purpose and definition of sponsorship. It has been my experience that, depending on where you are in the world, the concept of sponsorship varies and can range from philanthropy to sales promotion.

I have been asked by certain companies to recommend "philanthropic action programs" which turn out, on closer questioning, to be requests for event sponsorships that will gain wider recognition for the company or brand name. And, vice versa.

It must be stressed that the various forms and gradations of sponsorship do not make one better or more important than another. Each has its place, value and particular strengths which can help an organization achieve its goals. It is, however, of crucial importance to determine at the outset what those goals are, and which of the many forms of sponsorship is most likely to be right for your needs.

The second roadblock you will almost certainly encounter is the "CEO's pet". It can be intransigent and you may have to work around it or accommodate it and build around it. The CEO's pet may be a particular sport, branch of the arts or community or charitable activity. The CEO might see it as the most deserving of your company's support and even believe that it is the ideal vehicle to be the centerpiece of company sponsorship strategy. That might well be the case, but the chances are that there will be better ways of spending your sponsorship money. It will be up to you to navigate between the personal desires of your leader and the evidence produced by your investigations and analysis of the available opportunities. You will want as scientific a methodology as possible for identifying and prioritizing candidates for sponsorship. It allows for a rational discussion rather than a fight among a number of favorite events or causes, each with its own supporter.

The third hazard is the slick salesmanship of the organizations that own events or represent athletes and artists. You are likely to receive a torrent of applications for support from a range of agents, suggesting that you must not miss the once-in-a-lifetime opportunity to ensure your company is featured on the sleeve of an aspiring Formula 1 Grand Prix driver or a team that is about to be formed, or to support an attempt by someone wanting to make the first journey to the South Pole on roller blades.

Make sure you resist, at least until you have formulated your own sponsorship policy, decided how much you can afford and are completely ready to make a selection from several possible candidates.

Before you start this process, it is important to establish internally the role and goals of the activity to be planned. It will save misunderstandings and harsh post mortems.

Get clear what is expected by the key group of decision makers in your organization. You might find that one board member is expecting an activity that is quite altruistic and another something that will demonstrably improve the bottom line. Others will be in between. It is useful to list out for your interviews internally the range covered, as follows:

Pure philanthropy: This is the anonymous donation of money to charities, specifically nominated or via a distribution committee to worthy causes. The donor does not wish to have his name disclosed or to have any credit. According to an article in the *New York Times* of January 26, 1997, this kind of donation is declining and now represents a mere 3 per cent of charitable giving in the USA. Interestingly, the writer points out that the pressure to publicize the names of donors is not coming from donors themselves, many of whom are publicity shy, but from the recipients, such as hospitals and universities. They have discovered that the way to attract contributions is to publicize major gifts received from prominent people; this sets up a "top that" kind of competition among the rich, which swells the coffers of the luckier institutions. "To those that have, shall be given."

Posthumous philanthropy: Beware of the creation of a major trust fund by individuals who have accumulated exceptional wealth during their lifetime by methods that some might consider to have been excessively harsh and callous and, on occasion, unethical. Cynics dub this "conscience money". The trusts may be set up late in life or willed upon death. Some prominent trusts which have attracted notice because their independent boards have sometimes given money to causes and institutions that would have been anathema to the donor are The Ford Foundation, the Carnegie Foundation and The Rockefeller Foundation.

Smart philanthropy: There is, of course, truly altruistic posthumous philanthropy, too. This is a term used by organizations that want to build a bridge between charitable giving and self interest. In essence, this means they want to donate money (or services, or something else of value) to charitable causes that are strongly related, if possible, to their business and its goals. It is perhaps a new variant on the saying "charity begins at home". It can mean that there is some direct payback, not always in monetary terms; or it can mean that the organization is in a special position because of its own know-how or resources to offer help unavailable from any other sources.

■ Mobil

Mobil is a company that has been practicing smart philanthropy for decades, and long before the term itself was first used. But this element must be seen for what it is, one arrow in a quiver full of many forms of philanthropy.

To name just a few of Mobil's initiatives: Masterpiece Theater, a weekly TV broadcast of British drama on America's Public Broadcasting System which attracts a huge audience; annual publication of the Mobil Travel Guides, now a self-standing business in its own right with the guides established as the "bible" from which travelers and diners in the USA should pick places to stay and to eat; USA Track and Field Athletic Championships.

But it is in Mobil's sponsorship of carefully chosen arts and cultural projects that the keen observer can see just how smart Mobil's philanthropy can be. The company's selection of the subjects for sponsorship is anything but random. Each relates directly to a topic or region of interest to Mobil, often a place where it has important activities. It has sought to merge the interests and benefits to the communities in which it operates along with a public service and self interest. Examples are:

- Treasures of Ancient Nigeria: This exhibition of the remarkable bronze sculptures created in the Kingdom of Benin (province of Nigeria) was shown at the Royal Academy in London, the Metropolitan Museum of Art in New York and other major art venues. Mobil's initiative was appreciated by Nigeria's government as a valuable way of depicting the evolution of Nigeria's civilization and helped cement relations with this important source of oil production.
- Painters of the American West: The oilwell-owning Anschutz family of Denver had accumulated the USA's finest collection of "Western art" – paintings by such well-known artists as Remington. Mobil curated and exhibited a selection of these paintings at the Institute of Contemporary Arts in London with an opening ceremony performed by Prince Philip, Duke of Edinburgh. The show later toured to other venues. Shortly thereafter, it was announced that Mobil had acquired several oil wells from Anschutz.
- Patterns of the Hebrides: This was an exhibition commissioned from the photographer Gus Wylie at the time that Mobil was undertaking explorations in the North Sea and there was great concern for the environment by residents of the Hebrides and environmentalists at large. Gus Wylie's commission was to record on film the life and scenery before and after the completion of explorations and the laying of pipes. This would show Mobil's concern to return the islands to their

natural state, and the desired result was achieved. The exhibition, which toured, was opened in London by the Minister for Scottish Affairs.

■ Telecom

Another example of smart philanthropy is the creation of a consortium of major companies in the telecommunications industry to fund the attendance of representatives of less developed and newly developing countries at Telecom '95. The world's largest trade show and symposium, held every four years, Telecom in 1991 had raised eyebrows in many parts of the world for its display of opulence. One exhibitor's booth was an architectural wonder costing over $3 million. Critics said the event was becoming a rich man's club and was not affordable by many of the poorer nations.

The organizer of Telecom is the International Telecommunication Union (ITU), whose membership consists of 184 states and organizations from around the world. It is responsible for regulating, standardizing and developing telecommunications globally, as well as promoting a harmonious environment conducive to effective use of telecommunications products and services worldwide.

Formally affiliated with the United Nations, ITU has as one of its objectives to close the telecommunications gap between developed and developing countries. ITU decided to ensure that Telecom '95 would be open to the less developed and newly developing countries where the need for technological and infrastructure advance was greatest.

Financial contributions were solicited from 13 of the world's most prominent telecom companies – Alcatel, Cable & Wireless College, Ericsson, IBM, MCI Communications Corporation, Motorola, NEC, Northern Telecom, Nynex, Philips, Siemens, Telebras and TIA/USA. ITU created the Programme for Development with its mainstay a two-and-one-half day workshop for Least Developed Countries (LDCs) and Low Income Countries (LICs). This was the first such workshop and the first time giants of the fiercely competitive global telecommunications industry collaborated on such a joint project.

Though the telecommunications development gap between the affluent countries and the developing world has narrowed in recent years – LDCs and LICs account for more than 77 per cent of the world's populations, but only 5 per cent of the world's telephone lines – more than two-thirds of households around the world still have no basic telephone service.

According to the United Nations, the number of LDCs has increased from 25 in 1971 to 48 in 1994, and that figure will rise to 52 by 1999. Of the present 48 LDCs worldwide, 30 are in Africa, 13 in Asia-Pacific, 4 in the Arab Region and 1 in the Americas.

Titled "Human Resources and Technology", the workshop focused on these two areas of crucial importance for nations seeking to improve their telecommunication facilities and enhance their ability to operate efficiently in the rapidly changing telecommunications environment.

And, as the 200 delegates planned to upgrade their national telecom systems, you can be certain the 13 sponsor companies, all of them equipment suppliers, would be reminding them of their support for and participation in the ITU initiative. Smart philanthropy.

■ United Parcel Service

United Parcel Service is an example of an organization that seeks to use its special knowledge, resources and skills in its philanthropic outreach, rather than indiscriminately doling out contributions to a variety of causes, however noble. The UPS Foundation, the company's philanthropic arm, analyzes several charitable needs and agencies serving them, and then selects those which it feels it is in a unique position to help.

Throughout its 90-year history, UPS's strong commitment to community service clearly has been stated in its Corporate Mission Statement. In fact, one of the four subsections specifically addresses "Communities". UPS spreads the word, both internally and externally, that a fundamental element of its mission is to "build on the legacy of our company reputation as a responsible corporate citizen whose well-being is in the public interest and whose people are respected for their performance and integrity."

In 1988, The UPS Foundation reviewed research available at the time in an effort to help UPS better target philanthropic efforts. Illiteracy and hunger were identified as the two most urgent social challenges. UPS adopted these issues, contributing money and manpower through national and regional outreach efforts. For example, in 1988, UPS developed the Prepared and Perishable Food Rescue Program (PPFRP), which supports the growth and development of hunger relief programs. The company developed a technical services manual for new program start-ups and helped form FoodChain, a network of PPFRPs for shared information and resources. The precept was this: there are areas of the USA where food is scarce. There are other areas where there is an overabundance of food. UPS was able to use its unrivaled knowledge of transport and distribution systems to help the excess food get to the areas of need.

In 1989, UPS developed an adult literacy award program, which provides grants to programs that have proven effective in increasing basic literacy skills in the areas that the organizations serve. UPS expanded its literacy outreach to include education initiatives, including "school to work" and "welfare to work" initiatives in states where UPS has a strong presence, including Georgia, Kentucky, Illinois and Pennsylvania.

While UPS has strong relationships with national non-profit organizations such as the United Way and provides funding through the UPS Corporate Grants program, much of its charitable giving focuses on the individual UPS regions and programs developed by UPS. The primary focus for UPS is to support organizations in areas where UPS employees live and work. Each UPS region and district is responsible for making small contributions to local organizations, through the Corporate Charitable Contributions program.

In addition, UPS relies on one of its largest resources – its employees – to identify worthwhile local charities to receive grants and other donations. Through the UPS Region/District Grant Program, established in 1984, employees in each of the UPS domestic, Americas and Canada regions, the Corporate Office, the Air Group and Information Services recommend local non-profit organizations to receive grants of $100,000, $50,000 or $25,000.

Apart from monetary contributions, UPS's single largest contribution to non-profit organizations is its manpower. UPS is one of the largest employers in the US. Thousands of its employees have been giving back to the community – building and painting houses, cleaning up parks, teaching computer classes and hosting reading hours. So, in 1993, UPS organized this widespread network of volunteers into what is now the UPS Neighbor to Neighbor program. The goal was to increase the number of UPS employees who volunteer, and diversify their options. And, no dollar amount can be placed on the service that they provide.

Community philanthropy is natural for companies that were founded and have grown and prospered for many years in a particular place. As growth takes place, the city or town grows and the bonds between the company and the community strengthen. Often, that is the origin of schools, libraries, parks, buildings, streets, theaters, clubs and pools made possible by philanthropic support from the major local business enterprises.

Now, multinational companies, which are by definition also multilocal, need to approach the question of community philanthropy in a systematic fashion, as UPS has done in the way described earlier. Most consider it a very important element in establishing the newcomer company as one which intends to be a good corporate citizen and contribute to the community in which it is setting down roots.

The best policy is to take your time, study the balance of local politics on the one hand and make a careful list of the needs of the community on the other. Note those community activities that are already "owned" by other sponsors and discard them as prospects. Select one or two activities or needs which will gain the most credit among the local people. Has there been a long-term need for a swimming pool? A youth club? A day care center? Read the local press, talk to local people, listen to the debates at the local town hall meetings and pick the causes to support that will do the most good and enhance your reputation as a valued local citizen.

Community philanthropy is not just a question of giving cash. Equally important can be the personal commitment on the part of staff members or the donation of equipment or resources. An excellent and bold example of a multilocal community philanthropic initiative was that taken by AT&T in 1997 when it announced AT&T CARES, the most recent addition to its community service programs. This initiative encourages AT&T's 127,000 employees worldwide to devote one paid workday per year to their communities. According to the Points of Light Foundation, AT&T CARES is the largest publicly announced corporate volunteer program. It was launched in 16 states and Washington, DC, where AT&T volunteers helped a national charity, Second Harvest, collect food and set up a warehouse for its annual Thanksgiving Day food drive. It is estimated that AT&T CARES will represent a 1997 donation of one million hours, valued at approximately $20 million.

A complementary AT&T CARES grants program, initiated in 1994, reinforces employees' volunteer work. When an employee gives at least 50 hours of service annually to a non-profit group, he can request a $250 AT&T CARES grant, and when four or more employees volunteer at the same organization, they can combine their requests for a maximum grant award of $2,500. "By giving our time and money, we demonstrate not only our commitment, but also our conviction," says Marcy Chapin, the AT&T Foundation's vice president of community service programs. For example, Jenna McCaffrey and 20 AT&T colleagues, who are literacy coaches for academically at-risk elementary school students in Chicago's inner city, helped keep the tutoring project alive through an AT&T CARES grant.

Another AT&T initiative is The AT&T Learning Network, started in 1995, the most comprehensive technology donation ever made by an American company. It offers to connect all of the 110,000 US elementary and secondary schools to the Internet by the year 2000 and, in doing so, foster family involvement in education, provide professional development opportunities for teachers, and integrate technology training into the preparation of new teachers.

This scheme attracted a wave of favorable publicity in the national and international media. It has also created the framework for 127,000 opportunities to create good will at the local level – in addition to media stories – as each of AT&T's employees dedicates his charity day during each year.

The topic of community philanthropy is one of special importance to the international PR practitioner because customs vary from country to country. For most Japanese companies, corporate philanthropy was puzzling because it was not practiced in the same way as has become customary in the USA and other western democracies. Industry and commerce were seen to be intruding in the province of government agencies, the family and other societal organisms. For some time, this impeded the readiness of communities in other lands to accept Japanese companies as they established overseas branch operations, and that surely hampered the smooth path to growth and success.

After a while, Japanese, Korean and other Asian companies recognized philanthropy as part of the way of business life in their new markets and manufacturing locations and, as might be expected, they studied the topic very carefully. They sought and paid for the advice of philanthropic experts and public relations professionals on the correct way to begin. Now, even though the notion of corporate philanthropy is still foreign to them and is not practiced in the same way in the home market, Japanese and other Asian companies are among the most significant donors in the western world. **Cause-related marketing** stands at the halfway mark between philanthropy and sales promotion. This is the means by which companies can tie charitable giving to sales. In the broadest sense, cause-related marketing can be used to describe the activities of companies which are identified with certain causes or aspirations and which they promote to the public along with their products. A good example is The Body Shop, which achieved a worldwide reputation as an activist organization on behalf of the developing world and its peoples.

Through its buying policies and the way it made donations to less developed countries, as well as through its stated aims to be environmentally responsible, The Body Shop attracted a huge customer base among people who felt they were supporting these causes indirectly through their purchases. However, The Body Shop is also a cautionary tale of the man-traps and pitfalls awaiting companies with golden reputations. There are those who will not rest until they can show that the god others worship has feet of clay.

■ The Body Shop

The worldwide effect of a single negative thrust was demonstrated dramatically in the mid-1990s when the image of The Body Shop as an environmentally friendly and socially conscious cosmetics enterprise was shattered by an article in *Business Ethics*, a small Minneapolis journal. It laid out alleged details of corporate hypocrisy and exaggeration in the autumn of 1994, two years after a television documentary had charged the popular company with false claims about its position against animal testing.

In short order, publications all over the world reported contentions that The Body Shop, with 1,366 retail outlets worldwide, was actually just like its competitors; though highly regarded for being environmentally concerned, using pure materials of exotic origins and engaging in public-spirited programs, it was now accused of having exaggerated its claims, used chemicals tested on animals, bought very little or no natural materials from Third World countries, and done little charitable giving. Disgruntled former employees and franchisees came forward with more allegations of an "inside/outside" strategy: They said founder/CEO Anita Roddick, an iconoclastic marketing whiz, publicly attacked the so-called monsters of the cosmetics industry who continued to test product safety on laboratory animals, while at the same time her company used ingredients that had been animal-tested, and she admitted privately that such tests were essential.

The company's stock plunged. Senior staff members left, complaining of organizational problems. Overly fast expansion in the United States lost money. Anita Roddick and her husband, Gordon, co-founder and chairman, failed in their attempt to borrow money to take the company private and then turn it over to a non-profit foundation that would use profits to finance good works. Massive reorganization ensued, along with the hiring of Hill and Knowlton Public Relations.

Deep into its makeover, the company commissioned an independent audit which concluded that The Body Shop *had* maintained a strong social responsibility record and it refuted most of the criticism in the damning *Business Ethics* article. The study found, however, that the company's relationships with its external audiences had been poorly managed, particularly with shareholders and media, and it criticized response to customer and franchisee complaints. There had also been some exaggeration by The Body Shop in its communications materials about the environmental aspects of its products, the report said.

The global franchise corporation, which had started in 1976 in a tiny shop in Brighton and which had gone public in 1984, saw its stock ride high in 1992 but drop by 65 per cent four years later.

Fortune magazine in 1996 said it would "take years to tell whether the new marketing and sales strategies can turn around the company's fortunes" and counseled that "investors should probably stick to buying The Body Shop's soap but not its shares."

■ "Dolphin Safe" tuna

When the StarKist subsidiary of Heinz decided to end a consumer boycott of its canned tuna products by environmentalists by becoming the first company of its kind to establish a "Dolphin Safe" policy, which meant only buying products from fishing fleets that used nets that did not trap dolphins along with the tuna, it immediately won the loyalty of millions of people who had for long been identified with this cause. The results could be seen in an immediate surge of StarKist brand share against its rivals.

But the most obvious and measurable cause-related marketing programs directly link sales and philanthropy. Although it is commonly assumed that this is a technique that has only emerged over the past two decades, it has in fact been practiced for a long time by many corporations and other organizations.

■ Conservation coin

A fine example of cause-related marketing was a collaboration in the early 1970s between Spink, the famous London auction house specializing in numismatic coins, the Royal Mint and the World Wildlife Fund. This alliance created the World Wildlife Conservation Coin Collection, a series of coins issued by the 24 countries where a variety of creatures were threatened with extinction. Each country issued four coins, all of which were marketed on a worldwide basis to numismatic coin collectors. Care was taken to ensure the design of each coin was superb and the striking and polishing of each coin was to the highest standards, using the correct weights of gold and silver. In the sales literature, advertising and the public relations launch, it was made clear that a fixed proportion of the receipts from sales would go to help save the wildlife that was in peril. Buyers could, through their choices, indicate the animals they wanted saved because the person buying, for example, the four coins issued by Kenya, would be assured that his donation would go to that country.

■ Statue of Liberty

Jerry Welsh, when he was an executive at American Express, became the father of modern-day cause-related marketing, and Amex is a consistent and successful practitioner of the technique. The most famous example of the genre was the campaign to restore the Statue of Liberty, which was to celebrate its centennial in 1986 but had suffered structurally and decoratively. In short, "the lady", as the statue is affectionately known, needed a face lift, along with some even more radical reconstructive surgery. With no city, state or federal government eager to underwrite what was going to be an exceptionally costly undertaking, along came American Express as a white knight and savior of the statue that symbolizes the nation. How? The company pledged that it would donate one cent on every dollar for purchases charged to American Express cards, a dollar for every new card approved during the campaign period and a dollar for every $500 travel package purchased, toward the Statue of Liberty renovation fund. At the end of the promotion AMEX handed over a check for $1.7 million. They also undertook a major advertising and marketing campaign which helped attract other support for the renovation. Not only did American Express's sales volume increase, its reputation took a huge boost in America as a grateful nation celebrated the centennial. All the power of a skillful AMEX PR Department was deployed to make sure it was so.

More recently, American Express has had another cause. Charge Against Hunger is a campaign in which a percentage of all purchases made with the American Express family of cards is donated to charities devoted to feeding the hungry and homeless. Communications messages to members who use their charge cards for accommodation in hotels and splendid meals in restaurants make them easy prey for the promotion.

But American Express's larger rival in the payments system business, VISA, is also a major factor – internationally – in cause-related marketing, using its prime position as a "TOP" (Total Olympic Program) Worldwide sponsor of the Olympic Games as its key into this arena. "Pull for the Team" is an ingenious campaign that can be customized for use by VISA in every nation which participates in the Olympic Games. In this scheme, VISA pledges that a percentage of all charges billed to the VISA card at certain periods will be placed in a fund to help support the training and attendance of athletes of the nations concerned. As Summer and Winter Games approach and Olympic fervor becomes feverish, VISA benefits because people do their best to ensure their favorite athletes get a shot at winning gold.

■ Sponsorship

In the whole complex, costly and difficult-to-measure field of sponsorship, there is one rule to keep firmly fixed in mind from the outset, even at the evaluation stage of the various opportunities. It is the Iceberg Rule: the visible cost of the project is ALWAYS less than one third of the total final cost of a successful sponsorship.

A large number of new sponsors enter the field either not knowing this rule, or, having heard of it, believing that it only applies to sponsors other than themselves. They are wrong. The rule has no exceptions.

The visible part of the sponsorship is the price publicized by those who "own" an event, athlete, exhibition or team. In the case of the Olympic Games, the published cost of the highest level of Worldwide Sponsor was last recorded at $US48 million for a pair of games (Winter and Summer). But this merely represented the amount payable to the International Olympic Committee to obtain the rights to that title. To be sure, the purchase of those rights also came with attractive-sounding benefits, such as the right to use the Olympic rings in advertising and promotions, some free seats at the events and special rights to provide customer hospitality in the venues of the games.

But, in truth, the $48 million is a relatively small down payment, an entrance fee that opens up the chance for the sponsor to pay millions more to gain any real benefit from that down payment. Advertising, employee communications, sales promotion, public relations campaigns, all necessary to put the spotlight on an Olympic or any other sponsorship, always come extra.

■ Sponsorship selection

With sponsorship costs as high as they are, it is essential to select the right event, person or team to sponsor. This is where an objective scoring system pays huge dividends, especially because everyone believes they instinctively know the right choice – theirs.

The selection process you adopt – and there are many available – should start with a statement of the goal of the sponsorship. The goal of "creating wider awareness" of a corporate or brand name might call for a different vehicle from that which might meet the goal of "directly increasing sales and distribution" of a product or family of products.

The former goal will lead you to select an event which will attract a high level of media attention and will carry your name along with it. The second suggests a less widely publicized event but one where there are opportunities for offering hospitality to key distributors, or programs that allow for tie-ins at the retail level.

The other key consideration is the matching of the event with the brand or corporate identity strategy. There is little value in a sponsorship that has high visibility but has an irrelevant or unfortunate connection to the sponsoring company or brand.

■ Visa Olympics of the Imagination

An interesting example of a sponsorship within a sponsorship that helped reinforce brand identity is Visa's Olympics of the Imagination. This was created to offset an aggressive and sharp advertising strategy with a project that was warm, human and in the spirit of the Olympics, even though the Games had become overly commercialized and crowded with sponsors by the 1990s. In planning its agenda for the 1994 Games in Lillehammer, Norway, Visa International, the official worldwide payment system for the International Olympic Committee since 1986, needed to capitalize on its sponsorship in a way that would be global, good for business and sensitive to public perceptions.

The company had already initiated an association with art and culture during previous Olympic Games, by commissioning Olympic-themed art works from five prominent European artists. For 1994, Visa wanted to open the door to wider publicity opportunities, reflect the Olympic founding principle that sports should be blended with art, culture and education to enhance people's lives, and take note of the 100th anniversary of the International Olympic Committee.

Thus was born the award-winning Visa Olympics of the Imagination, developed with Edelman Public Relations Worldwide. An invitation would be issued to talented, artistic youth in many countries, to submit images they thought represented the 2094 Games. Ultimately, Norway, Canada and the United States were chosen as venues for the competition that would produce 25 young winners who would attend the Lillehammer Games and whose art works would be exhibited there.

It was most important that the program would be internationally implemented but adapted to local market needs. The campaigns in the US, Canada and Norway were anything but the same.

In the US, daily newspapers in ten major markets partnered the campaign by advertising the contest and printing entry forms, distributing posters and 50,000 Olympics information kits to schools, judging entries and honoring the winners at special events and in more advertising.

Publicity came in three waves: the kick-off and call for entries, announcing the winners, and covering their departure for Norway.

The Norwegian program partner was Sparbanken Nor, one of the country's largest banks and an Olympic sponsor, which promoted the art competition and offered entry materials in its branches. The Oslo International Children's Art Museum participated in the judging and was the site of the press conference to announce the winners.

In Canada, Visa partnered the Canadian Olympic Association (COA), in cooperation with the ten provincial and two territorial departments of education, enabling the Visa program materials to be inserted in school packets distributed by the COA. Canadian school rules restricting commercial programs made this partnership critical and enabled the Visa of the Imagination contest to be positioned as an integral part of the Olympic Resource Kit distributed in 15,000 private and public elementary schools.

In addition to the publicity and attention Visa gained in the three countries, significant visibility was garnered at Lillehammer, through the centrally situated, high-traffic exhibit of the 25 winner's entries and related VIP events. The invitational opening of the art exhibit and dinner drew the highest-level Olympic officials. The winners were invited to participate in the opening ceremonies of the Games. Members of the Canadian Bobsled Team, the US Ski Team and the Norwegian Cross Country Ski Team came to the exhibition tent to have their portraits painted by the young artists.

Upon its conclusion, the Visa program had generated stories read, heard or seen by 300 million people globally, always with a positive portrayal of the company. More than 7,000 youths had submitted art works and the winners were a compelling group who were naturals for publicity efforts. Visitors to the art exhibit at Lillehammer numbered more than 100,000. About 125,000 special-edition postcard reproductions of the art works were distributed, in two or three languages, as invitations and announcements.

The 1994 Visa Olympics of the Imagination won a Golden World Award from the International Public Relations Association, a Big Apple Award from the Public Relations Society of America/NY Chapter, and a Creativity in Public Relations Award from the publication *Inside PR*.

Two years later, for the Centennial Atlanta Games, the well-tested program expanded to 20 countries, including South Africa, Japan, Israel, Australia, The Netherlands, Canada and the US. It had a site on the Internet, international distribution of point-of-sale materials through Visa merchants and banks, strong media partnership and coverage in the US, and school materials in nine languages going to 50,000 schools worldwide.

■ Process

For the international PR practitioner, the selection process is all the more complex with a matrix of different cultures, sporting interests and local managements all making a choice, or even choices, very hard. This is where a disciplined selection process pays the most dividends. A good process will help you decide whether you will get greater benefit from investing in one of the multi-million-dollar global sponsorships available, such at the Olympics or the Soccer World Cup; or from a mosaic of smaller local sponsorships. The attractions of each approach (and some major sponsors with plenty to spend take both roads) are easy to see. A company that was an important and thoughtful early sponsor on a multi-national basis was Gillette. It saw very early – in the 1960s – that sports sponsorship was an effective and powerful promotional weapon, and it was the first commercial sponsor of cricket in England.

The Gillette Cup, started in 1963, was not only the first commercialization of the game but the birth of a new form of the game, one-day competitions, a development that has since ensured the continued success of cricket as a spectator sport in the new commercial age.

This sponsorship was not a random selection. To be sure, for the modern television era, cricket needed a new injection of money, promotion and the creation of a new, less lengthy format than the usual three-, five- or six-day matches. Gillette was there to help and to gain the benefits. But this was just one example of a worldwide sponsorship policy in which the company had set its own rule: It would sponsor the national sport of each country where it conducted a sizable business, thus demonstrating its local corporate citizenship and also winning over local customers for its products. The Baseball World Series in the USA, Gillette Cup Cricket in England, Pelota in South Africa and other similar sponsorships combined into a coherent global sponsorship policy.

For the international company, it is important to involve regional and local managements in the selection and planning process of any sponsorship. Early participation pays dividends later on, in the form of enthusiastic implementation of the agreed programs.

It might also help to reshape the global sponsorship policy. Many companies now have several levels of sponsorship ranging from the mega global effort (such as the Olympics) to subsidies for small local events.

■ Multilayered sponsorships

Rank Xerox was an early and clever exponent of the multilayered sponsorship policy. At the national level in major markets, such as the UK, they would select one or more high-profile events to sponsor. At one time it was the Slazenger Golf Tournament, which offered a combination of awareness through name association in media advertising, poster and public relations as well as superb hospitality opportunities for their major customers.

At the same time, the Rank Xerox headquarters required each of its regional units in the United Kingdom to allocate a certain sum of money for local sponsorships. It also required a report and rationale for the selection of the events and the plans for maximizing the return on investment in the sponsorship through ads, PR, etc.

Each regional unit picked events that were very local and important to the communities in which they operated – the Scottish Opera was one selection for the Scottish Region – so that the company became a welcome member of the local business circles in each of the principal cities where their customers were situated. Guidelines were given and experiences were exchanged, but there was no requirement for the money to be directed to any particular sport or branch of the arts. The only requirement was that the money allocated should be spent, and spent wisely.

■ Sponsorship criteria

For any major international corporation to plan, manage and implement an effective global sponsorship program, there needs to be a common commitment to work within an agreed set of criteria. Here is a suggested list.

Every sponsorship activity *must*:

- Express agreed brand or corporate values
- Approach audience targeting systematically
- Create an opportunity for direct contact with specific audience groups
- Have sufficient impact on a wide scale in order to be visible to individuals not directly engaged with the sponsorship activity
- Demonstrate synergy across all operating regions/countries
- Show your company's edge against its competitors. For this, you must have the broadest possible exclusivity within your product/industry category and be able to play an active part in the development of the sponsored activity. This means influencing and approving the way your organization's involvement is presented and communicated
- Allow your products, services and technology to play an active part in the development of sponsored activity and offer a contribution or benefit to the sponsored party
- Be exploited actively and aggressively in order to extend the value of the sponsorship package

Make a 'no go' list of events that might be offensive or controversial because they might be considered discriminatory, violent, immoral, unethical, antagonistic or environmentally harmful. Do not sponsor religious groups or political organizations, issues or activities, with the exception of those issues or organizations that are indisputably humanitarian or directly related to your business activities.

Table 11.1 EDELMAN 100-POINT M.U.S.T. S.ystem[SM]

Edelman M.U.S.T. S.ystem Element	Scoring	Score (100 point max.)
Media Appeal Does the program generate news about the company, brand, retailers, etc.? – Nationally: consumer; trade/business media – Locally: consumer; trade/business media	20 points	
User Friendliness Is the program flexible and easy to implement? Does it encourage participation among: – Consumers – Trade – Salesforce	15 points	
Sales Appeal Does it reach out and "sell" the brand in a unique way? Does it differentiate the brand from the competition among: – Consumers – Salesforce – Brand Management – Trade	20 points	
Thematic Applications Does it identify the brand "spirit"? Does it make participants feel good about being involved?	15 points	
Special Event Potential Does it offer opportunities that increase reach; impact; duration in market?	15 points	
Bonus Points Does it offer extra benefits such as brand imagery? Does it elevate brand from clutter?	(+/–)15 Points	
TOTAL SCORE (100 points maximum)		

EDELMAN 100-POINT M.U.S.T. System Measurement Standard	
Superior Program	95–100
Excellent	90–94
Good	85–89
Fair	76–84
Don't Bother	75 or less

■ Evaluation scoring systems

There are many evaluation scoring systems to help the potential sponsor weigh the competing offerings. You can also make up your own system with weightings that are highly relevant to your particular case. I show here the proprietary system developed by my own company over several years of involvement in this special field. It rates six potential elements of a successful sales promotion/public relations program, as viewed from the PR perspective.

■ Post-event evaluation process

As important as the pre-evaluation process is the post-event evaluation.

I suggest you use the same format as for the Edelman M.U.S.T. System – just to make sure the musts were not "maybes".

In addition, qualitative and quantitative research should be undertaken.

■ Quantitative:

- How many people were aware of your sponsoring involvement? This measurement will be gleaned from audience ratings (if broadcast), gate/attendance ratings (if an exhibit/exhibition), entry numbers (if a competition), clip numbers (if magazine based), etc.
- Cost per thousand. This measurement will be determined by calculating the overall cost of the sponsorship program for each thousand individuals reached.
- Optionally, try to calculate the level of increased business which will have been directly influenced by the sponsorship.

■ Qualitative:

- Through focus groups, establish the match between audience expectation, lifestyles, or mindset and the sponsorship personality; rate positive feedback from the demographic and psychographic groups of importance to you.
- Through telephone interviews, establish awareness and favorability of the sponsorship program with specific audience groups (consumers, channels, operators, business partners), as well as with employees.

CHAPTER 12

The Infrastructure of your Organization

Finding the right structure for a PR department is one of the hardest tasks facing the head of communications in a global corporation.

And when you think you have a superb plan with all your personnel needs identified and a really workable structure laid out on paper, you are still at the bottom of the mountain.

I learned this when I was asked to analyze the existing PR structures and resources and assess future needs at the Basel headquarters of Hoffman La Roche. At the end I was expected to prepare a plan and present it to the chairman, Mr. Fritz Gerber.

In addition to the extraordinarily interesting professional challenges presented by undertaking this assignment for one of the world's most successful companies with a pronounced corporate culture, the arrangements made to enable me to conduct my work efficiently added an extra layer of interest.

The assignment called for my presence "on site" to conduct interviews with board members and senior management. I also had to observe the PR operations in action and conduct a communications audit of all materials produced. To do this, I was provided with the office of Dr. Adolf W. Jann, Mr. Gerber's predecessor as chairman. It was of a size and furnished in the manner that you might expect for one of Switzerland's leading companies, which at the time boasted the world record share price and produced the top selling drug, Valium. A single Roche share was worth close to US$100,000.

The windows gave onto a courtyard where a gleaming white Henry Moore sculpture sat resplendent on a manicured green lawn with perfect edges. This was testimony indeed to a long line of effective and financially rewarding medications produced by the company which spent more on its research and development than any other pharmaceutical company.

Working from the retired chairman's office immediately signaled to everyone within Roche that the work I was doing was of the highest importance. All doors were open and I was given full cooperation in my task.

It was however, a somewhat eerie experience. To work from Dr. Jann's office was one thing. But it was exactly as he had left it. His pencils and pens on the desk. His books on the shelves. Various gifts and souvenirs on the occasional tables. Photos of his family on the desk and shelves. At first I felt an impostor, but as no one else, including the secretarial staff in this exclusive office area where the top directors worked, thought anything of it, I soon got used to it and it became my temporary "home".

On completion of my study, a meeting was arranged with Mr. Gerber, the chairman. He listened attentively, his sharp intellect somehow advertised in his eyes, as I described the structure I proposed Roche adopt to handle corporate communications in the future. My recommendations had carefully written job descriptions for each of the important positions and the whole plan was illustrated by the necessary organization chart (organigram, as it is known in most European countries) with a solitary box at the top of the Christmas tree for the Head of Corporate Communications.

Mr. Gerber peered at this intently and then asked a single question: "Who has this position?"

I replied by saying we needed to hire that person and then outlined the qualifications needed and the briefing that I had written for the executive search. It was a top job and needed a renaissance man (or woman).

Mr. Gerber closed the meeting: "Let me meet that person when you have found him and I will tell you if the whole thing will work, or not."

Of course he was right. In a profession such as public relations, the human factor is all-important. A technically correct organizational structure is doomed if it has the wrong person at the pinnacle. But then, that is true of any organization, military unit or government department.

It is just as true that a superb leader of a major company's corporate communications needs a structured team if he is to accomplish anything worthwhile.

So assuming that Mr. Gerber – or your own CEO – thinks that he has the right leader for corporate communications, what kind of departmental organization structure is "best practice" and what size should it be? What kind of talents should the employees have? Where should they be located? What reporting lines are solid and what are "dotted line"?

There may be studies and reports on this but they cannot possibly be conclusive. In my experience the range of sizes and structures among various companies is so wide and disparate that they do not lead you to any kind of "norm".

■ Big vs. modest

At one end of the scale stands a company like AT&T before 1996, when a major staff reduction program got under way. The public relations department had over 800 employees, 8 with the title of vice president or higher, more than 25 with the title director and 600 or 630 with the title manager. The majority were based in the United States. One wag was heard to suggest that the media be notified of a new toll free (Freephone) number with which to get information from the company – 1-800 ATT PROS.

This number of people reflected a commitment to public relations by the company, which had started decades earlier when it was the cornerstone of the Bell Telephone System, of which the legendary Arthur Page was director of public relations from 1927–1946. Communications with its customers, the public, the communities it served and the lawmakers whose understanding and votes were needed to expand telephony were a top priority in the company. While 800 PR staffers might seem a huge number to some who are trying to manage with a very small department, it only represents one PR person for 100,000 customers, a ratio that is exceeded by many other companies.

Moreover, AT&T had a philosophy rooted in its history as a public service utility, which demanded (by law, as well a simple business judgment) onerous obligations for disclosure, dialogue and public debate.

At the other end of the spectrum, there are a few companies like United Parcel Service which has twice as many employees as AT&T and half the revenues, and which manages its global public relations with a team of no more than 16 executives in-house, not including those involved in employee communications and public affairs. And no less than ten years ago, before the 80-year-old company undertook its twin initiatives of modernization and globalization, it had fewer than half a dozen PR officers and no agency of record.

Both companies augment their department with the assistance of PR agencies.

There is little point in suggesting that the ideal size for a PR department is 408 people (the average of the total staffs of those two companies). That would be nonsense. But it is surprising to me how many people believe there is a model department that can be taken off the shelf and will fit any company with some minor alterations.

There are, however, some basic principles, a few alternatives and different combinations of resources.

The trick is to fit the structure to your own needs after you have analyzed them carefully. No one model is necessarily better than another. But it might be a better fit and therefore work better for you.

■ The functional model

The functional structure is probably the original model for major corporations, quite commonly in use in the 1950s–1970s and still to be found in quite a number of companies. This model (see Chart 12.1) usually features a single executive who is responsible for all company communications, which he undertakes with the assistance of various functional departments. There might be a press officer whose sole duties are the production of press releases and contact with the media. Sometimes that assignment is kept in the hands of the senior officer and the press officer is only concerned with the production of the news material and its distribution.

The arrangement is quite usual in Europe where the major companies have executives nominated to the position of "speaker or spokesman". The spokesman issues company statements and gives comments. In the unofficial links with the media, journalists know that only the "spokesman's" comments can be quoted as the company's official viewpoint, even though they may have gleaned information from others in the company. This arrangement can also be seen at work in various government institutions where the spokesman gives the daily briefing on important matters.

A second unit is a publications department which is often under the management of a person with a journalistic background. Here are written and produced the various documents any company needs: employee magazines and newsletters, customer newsletters, the annual report, brochures etc.

Sometimes linked to the publications department, but often separate, is a graphics production unit which might maintain a studio of commercial graphic artists, photographers (with darkroom) film cameramen and videographers. There is the

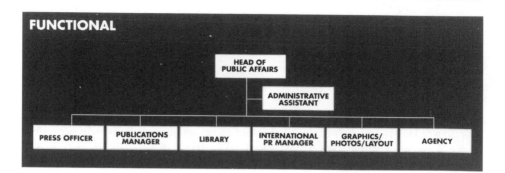

Chart 12.1

ability in such units to produce finished art and occasionally there is the addition of an in-house printing facility able to produce to a high standard and in some quantity.

A library, or archive, is also maintained to store the materials produced.

If the company operates internationally, there is usually an international PR officer charged with the task of working with the international media, usually through local press officers in the subsidiaries or their locally hired agencies.

An agency is invariably retained in such structures because a strong production capability is not always matched by a strong general or specialist counseling capability and the wider pool of skills among agency executives can be called upon as needed.

This functional model has become outdated as "headcount reduction" and "outsourcing" have become the magical management mantras of the moment. Moreover, with the high speed at which technology has changed the production processes of graphic design and artwork, printing and cinematography, most companies do not want to risk equipment investments which might be outdated the day they are installed. Most countries have now spawned a host of large and small organizations specialized in each of these production techniques and their services can be contracted at excellent prices.

■ The quadrant

It is the dream of a serious and ambitious public relations practitioner to be directly responsible for the management of what I describe as the Communications Quadrant.

The Communications Quadrant is shown in the illustration 12.2 which also indicates the function in which the communications representative is most usually based and his direct line reporting. In most corporations today, he will have a greater or lesser degree of input on all four sections depending on the character and territoriality of other members of the executive Board.

In some companies, all the communications executives in each quadrant report directly to the chief communications officer (CCO) or head of public relations and have a dotted line relationship with the managers of the staff departments concerned (chart 12.3).

In such a model the CCO reports directly to the CEO of the company and will almost certainly be a member of the executive committee or board of the company, along

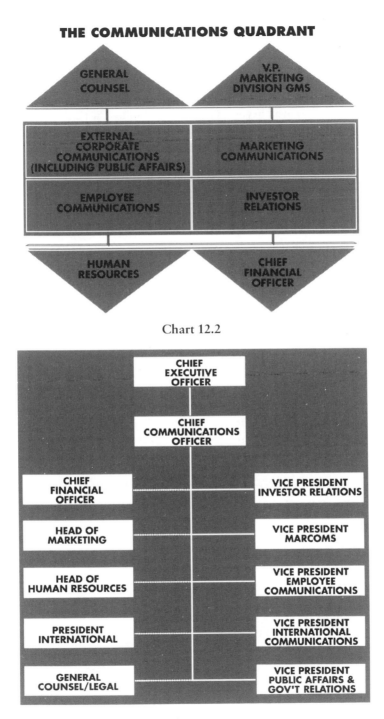

THE COMMUNICATIONS QUADRANT

Chart 12.2

Chart 12.3

with the general counsel or chief legal officer, the chief financial officer, the head of marketing and the head of human resources.

This schematic is, however, quite rare in my experience. More common is a structure in which the most senior public relations professional reports to the CEO, and maintains a close relationship with him and in the decision-making processes of the management committee. But he will have only a very small staff reporting to him – and sometimes no staff at all beyond a personal assistant. The people in charge of each branch of communications report directly to the senior officer of each function. Thus, the vice president of investor relations is directly employed by the chief financial officer but will maintain a dotted line reporting relationship with the chief communications officer.

■ Study of 100 companies

A major benchmarking survey conducted in 1997 by Edelman Public Relations Worldwide, The Medill School of Journalism and Opinion Research Corporation, sheds some light on how companies organize themselves to handle corporate communications. One hundred international companies participated. Here are some of the more interesting findings about reporting lines and infrastructure:

- Sixty per cent of top communications officials are at the vice president/vice chairman level. Nearly 2 in 10 hold the title of director, and 1 in 10 are senior vice presidents. The remaining 13 per cent hold the following titles: manager (8 per cent), corporate vice president (3 per cent) and executive vice president (2 per cent).
- The senior-most communicators report directly to the CEO at 54 per cent of the companies surveyed. For those communicators who do not report directly to the CEO, 30 per cent report to the vice president, senior vice president or vice chair level of the organization.
- Regardless of direct lines of reporting, 93 per cent, nearly two-thirds of the most senior communicators, counsel with the CEO at least weekly and 15 per cent counsel with the CEO on a daily basis.
- The senior-most corporate communications positions are generally held by highly-educated individuals. Approximately one-quarter hold post-graduate degrees, with another quarter holding graduate degrees. Of the remaining half, 44 per cent report a four-year degree, with the remaining responses indicating "some college" or "other" education.
- In addition to the educational demographic breakdown, the professional demographics of this group are as follows. More than 50 per cent come from a public relations background, with the next most commonly reported categories, marketing and finance, ranking only 7 per cent each. The remaining responses were scattered among a wide variety of professions.

Although survey respondents returned a variety of functional communications areas for which senior-most communicators are primarily responsible, the core public relations functions are much better represented at this senior level than are other areas such as advertising or marketing. Nearly one-third of these senior-most communicators have corporate communications as their primary functional responsibility, followed by public relations (16 per cent) and public affairs (12 per cent).

The range of specific functions which fall under the corporate communications umbrella is becoming more diverse. More than 4 in 10 report that corporate communications maintains final oversight for advertising, marketing and promotional activities. Surprisingly, more than 10 per cent are also directly responsible for customer service at their respective organizations.

CORPORATE COMMUNICATIONS RESPONSIBILITIES

Media Relations	99%
Crisis/Issues Management	93%
Employee Communications	88%
Corporate Identity/Image	83%
Financial Communications/Investor Relations	75%
Research & Measurement	75%
Community Relations/Corporate Philanthropy	74%
Advertising, Marketing & Promotions	43%
Government Affairs	35%
Customer Service	11%

Chart 12.4

Nearly 9 in 10 respondents indicate the use of external communications agencies at corporate headquarters, with more than 7 in 10 also using external agencies at the discretion of each business unit. Further, more than 5 in 10 also employ external communications agencies within their various geographic regions. Only 5 per cent do not use outside communications agencies.

Overall, the annual operation budget (excluding salaries) for corporate communications activities was reported as follows:

GLOBAL CORPORATE COMMUNICATIONS BUDGET

[US$ equivalent]:

Less than $1 million	25%
greater than $1 million, but less than $5 million	39%
greater than $5 million, but less than $10 million	11%
greater than $11 million, but less than $15 million	4%
greater than $20 million	15%

Chart 12.5

It is customary for most companies to draw a clear line between communications in the "home country" of operations and in international operations, with one person assigned to be responsible for management of communications in non-domestic markets.

This rule is true for most multinationals, whether the home base is in the UK, USA, Germany, Switzerland, Sweden, Netherlands or France.

It has yet to be seen if this will change as some multinationals aspire to grow into global corporations and the distinctions between domestic and foreign markets disappear.

■ Separate role for international PR

Meantime there are good practical reasons why the separate role of the international PR manager within corporations continues to exist:

*   Most companies have a long history in their own communities and know their way around the local and national media, the influential groups important for the business, their political representatives and their customers. They are less certain of themselves in their overseas markets, which vary widely in almost every respect. An international PR manager who makes it his business to be knowledgeable about these markets and can manage a network of widely dispersed PR representatives is worth his weight in gold.
*   As a rule, the chief communications officer at corporate HQ has to be intensely involved in certain aspects of his function that are of lesser importance overseas. Investor relations might be necessary in various markets where the company's stock is listed and traded but it remains essentially something that is conducted from HQ. It is still true that the large majority of shares of even the most global companies are owned by people in the "home" country. Similarly, human resources and regulatory affairs have a heightened importance in the home market of most companies, which means that unless there is a senior person responsible for the international component and an active advocate for action, the pressures of the home market can leave international communications as the Cinderella.
*   While the home market pressures place its needs uppermost in the minds of top management in many countries, it is especially the case with many American corporations. This is not just tradition or a way of thinking, it is also a matter of size. The average major corporation in the USA (excluding public utilities which have traditionally served local communities) is likely to have 80 per cent of its sales in its home market, a factor of its great population, wealth and appetite for consumption. For the Swiss or Dutch multinational, the motto "export or die" (or, more likely nowadays, "establish overseas subsidiaries to make and sell") is apt. In both cases the home market is likely to represent less than 10 per cent of the potential. So the need for the smaller nations to achieve the right formula for overseas communications is that much greater.

- The qualifications of the international PR manager might be quite different from those of an executive who needs only to operate in the home market. Some of these qualities are described in chapter 1. Briefly, he will need to be culturally aware, patient, open minded and inquisitive about alien customs and government procedures, with the ability to work with people from a variety of nations.
- At the same time, the international executive must never become detached from the "mother company" and totally concentrate on the non-domestic operations. One vital role is to act as a bridge to the PR staff overseas who need and rely on him to be their link to headquarters, the conduit of policies and news (never underestimate how most employees who work a great distance from headquarters feel starved of information). Finally, he is the coach and inspiration who transfers that most indefinable but, arguably, most important element: the corporate culture.

■ PR aligns with main structure

The public relations organizational structure must be aligned with the main management structure of the business.

If there is a total devolution of authority to national operating units, the PR arrangements must reflect this. If the company manages through a highly disciplined

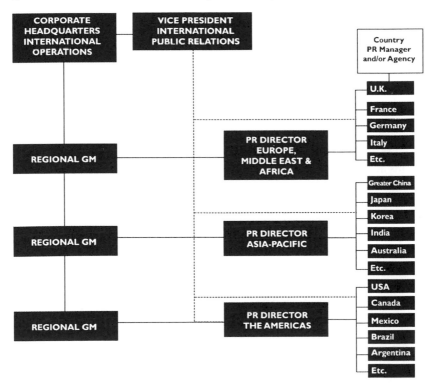

Chart 12.6

network of regional control centers which in turn manage the national operating units, then the PR department should provide a matching interface. If most authority is centralized at headquarters, PR will follow suit.

Given a general business trend in which companies break the world into geographic regions, it is now very common for PR departments to organize along the same lines. The organization of the world into trading blocks (e.g. the European Union, North American Free Trade Agreement, Association of South East Asian Nations) along with the wish to keep costs down by doing certain tasks at a regional level rather than many times over at national level, are just two of the factors driving this trend.

A typical regional structure is shown in chart 12.6.

In practice, the VP of international public relations usually maintains a close liaison with the regional PR directors and may well have been the most important person in their selection. For geographical and structural reasons in most companies, the direct reporting line is to the regional general manager, or his appointee; at the operational level, dual management exists. The same slightly "blurred" reporting lines exist between the regional PR director and the country PR manager (or agency), which is really in the front line of the action. In this case and almost every case where consumer products companies are concerned, the solid line is usually with the general manager of the operating subsidiary.

■ Agency support

The idea that companies make a choice between installing an in-house PR system or using a consultancy/agency is no longer valid.

The majority of companies nowadays combine external and internal resources. Of those responding to the Edelman/Medill/ORC benchmarking survey 95 per cent said they retained agencies to work in concert with internal staff.

Companies which started their international expansion early and had established a network of overseas subsidiaries began to recognize the importance of public relations in the early 1960s, some time after they had established a system to handle their international advertising needs. This was one reason why, in the case of the major American corporations, public relations usually started as a service outgrowth from their (American-owned) advertising agencies. The advertising agencies served clients whose creative work – the advertisements themselves – was identical in every market around the world, save for a change of language. Tampax was one such company, and the policy seems to have worked. The negative side was that the ad agency's subsidiaries in the various markets had nothing to do other than to place the order for ad space and deliver the artwork which had been prepared in New York.

Many of the ad agency networks that are now huge worldwide operations thus built their networks on the commissions earned from their home-based clients, going into local markets to serve their needs.

The pattern established by the Americans in the '60s was later emulated by the Europeans (Saatchi & Saatchi), starting with their stable of loyal British clients, and the Japanese (Dentsu), with their marquee brand names. Each of the ad agency networks spawned or bought a PR agency to fill out the service offering to their clients.

However, thus far, advertising agencies have not shown themselves to have been successful as managers of PR operations.

In other cases an enormous degree of autonomy was conferred on the local subsidiary which selected its own advertising – and PR – agency or exercised total control over the work of the corporate agency branch in the local country.

In some cases the independence was so extreme that brand and corporate identities of certain companies grew far apart and lost strength.

Over the years four basic agency relationship structures have become the most commonly used.

■ The worldwide agency of record

For many clients – not to mention agencies – the ideal relationship they seek to achieve is one in which there is a single agency retained. The agency has to provide an identical match of skills at the corporate head office and in each of the worldwide markets in which the client company operates.

In the mature commercial world that now exists, companies seeking to make such an arrangement will almost certainly have a great deal of tidying up to do, dismantling myriad individual agency relationships that have grown up over the years.

The advantages sought by the clients that want to go this route are:

- Size, which will bring a high level of commitment by the agency, access to its top talent and a readiness on the part of the agency to invest in areas of importance to the client, but that otherwise might not have been a priority.
- Exclusivity. A financially sizable multi-faceted relationship will provide the client with leverage to assure the agency is not available in any place to serve the client's competitors.
- Efficient contact procedures. If the agency provides a limited number of points of contact and undertakes to manage the day-to-day aspects of the programs, the client has relieved himself of a huge amount of work.
- Budget control and centralized billing. If the system works well, administrative time for the client and his staff working through bills from a large number of different agencies, all presented in different formats, will be avoided.
- Staff management. When things go wrong, as they undoubtedly will from time to time, or when a member of the agency staff is not performing adequately, the problem can be raised centrally, saving the client the unpleasant task of seeking to make a personnel change with a local agency manager.

Although such a global agency-of-record relationship might seem like nirvana for the chief corporate communications officer of a global enterprise, it is also fraught with problems of implementation.

- Gaps on the map and in PR specialties. There are few agencies that can offer clients matching global coverage in all their markets although a single handful, my own among them, are represented in the principal business centers of the world. If the geographic spread is adequate, the expertise in specialist PR skills – Public Affairs, Investor Relations, Marketing Communications – might have some blank spots. Even if all these factors show up well on the first screening, it will be the greatest good luck if the agency is completely free from potential conflicts. The client might also find that he is not equally impressed with the agency's capabilities or creativity in all markets or specialties.
- Inadequate strategic competence and coordination. Although the agency might demonstrate to the client sufficient dots on the map and experts in all the specialist fields of importance, the "chemistry" and added-value judgment provided by the top client service manager may be considered lacking; there might be real difficulties in getting the agency groups to work effectively as a team – among themselves and with the client.

If for any of these reasons it seems undesirable for client or agency to establish a global relationship, then a number of alternatives are available, and in today's marketplace for PR they are in the majority.

■ Strategy and core program development

It is now quite usual in the pharmaceutical and technology sectors for global companies to engage the services of a PR agency to develop core programs for the world launch or roll-out of new products.

The work product is a detailed plan (not unlike an architect's blueprint for a new building). The client and its retained agencies in various markets, or agencies hired for the specific project, implement the plan with adaptation in markets around the world. The selection of the local agencies is the responsibility of the local subsidiary or affiliate of the client. The local office of the agency, if it has the necessary skills, is usually on the selection short list. In such cases, full responsibility for the management and coordination of the program is firmly in the hands of the client company. It can mean that many agencies which are highly competitive with each other are required to work in harmony.

■ Agencies with regional responsibilities

Some clients are now forging agency relationships based on regional responsibilities. They feel that, although it might be impossible to find a single agency that can serve their needs worldwide, they can make exclusive arrangements region by region, with perhaps one agency responsible for strategic development and core programs.

For example, the giant Korean chaebol (conglomerate) Samsung has gone this route. Its corporate PR agency of record in Japan is Hakuhodo, in Europe Shandwick and in the other regions of The Americas, Greater China and South East Asia the agency is Edelman Worldwide.

■ The piebald network

There are many instances of clients that are very nearly able to establish a full worldwide network in partnership with an agency and a compromise is reached in which a minority of network offices are drawn from independent local firms or the local branch of a multinational agency. There can be any number of reasons for this, including the following. An otherwise strong international agency might have a few weak spots in markets of importance to the client; it is mutually agreed that, if the agency cannot strengthen its operation, the client is best served by seeking alternative counsel and assistance. It might be the global agency has no representation in a market; or the client company has an excellent historical relationship with a local agency which it wishes to continue. In such circumstances, I believe that most reputable global agencies welcome the addition of the "non-family" agencies into the network and soon operate quite well as a team.

■ The cherry-picked network

Some senior international PR practitioners favor the so-called "cherry picking" method of agency selection to form an international network. In fashion in the 1950s and '60s, this ideal-sounding way of selecting the best candidate agency in each market and forming a superb network is much harder now, and is fraught with landmines.

First, it places a huge burden of time, responsibility and administration on the client's most senior communications professional, in an era of drastically reduced PR department manpower. Few now have the chance to tour the world in leisurely fashion, interviewing candidate firms.

Second, the chances are strong that a well-established local firm will be eliminated through conflict.

Fine local firms are also candidates for acquisition, and many client companies which have "cherry picked" a network with great success find that it is short lived; a local agency is often bought or merged with another, which changes the relationship and might even end it if the merger partner serves a rival client.

■ The agency implant

There is one other option to be considered when structuring a public relations department and network, and that is an agency implant or executive on loan.

This was a service model pioneered by Carl Byoir in the years immediately following the end of World War II and was hugely successful, propelling his agency into becoming the largest in America. Instead of serving clients from staff largely based in the agency premises and working on more than one client engagement at a time, Byoir assigned executives to clients on a full-time basis and situated them at the clients' offices. The arrangement almost guaranteed that Byoir came out with a profit and that the client received a specified level of service. The implant system is gaining in favor once again, but for different reasons. In the strange world of corporate logic, a budget for an agency might be tight but funds might be found to support a contracted executive who cannot be hired as an employee, with agency profit margin built in.

The loaned executive is also an ideal solution for engagements which are known in advance to be short, and adding to the permanent staff would make no sense.

Other instances in which implants are useful are when a member of the permanent staff leaves and it will take time to find a replacement; or when a staffer must take a leave of absence for health reasons. In such cases, the agency might be able to assign an executive fully experienced in that client's program, who could step into the breach and fill the position on a temporary basis.

CHAPTER 13

The Public Relations Agency[*]

The public relations consultancy business (or counseling, as it is known in the USA) is one of the fastest-growing businesses. There is every prospect that this growth will continue.

■ History

The description "consultancy" or "agency", depending on the country concerned, was applied to the firms, individuals, partnerships and companies that established themselves in practice in the early years following the Second World War. At that stage the larger part of the services offered to clients consisted of practical implementation of public relations tactics and there was less emphasis on the analysis of problems and the supply of advice alone, than is the case nowadays. Because several of the early post-war practitioners had a background in journalism – although by no means all of them – the element of consulting and advice grew out of their special knowledge of the working of the media, the correct way to present a story for publication and a feeling for the way in which the public might react to publicity in the media. A few individuals stand out as major formative figures in the establishment of the public relations consulting and agency profession on an international basis. Marion Harper, the creator of Interpublic, based on the international network of McCann Erickson advertising agencies, was an important figure. McCann at one time had what I believe was the largest international PR operation, which operated under the name Infoplan. Its principal offices were in the USA, UK, Germany and France. (A sister company, Marplan, was a force in the world of international market research.)

Tim Traverse-Healy built Infoplan into the powerhouse of its time, an early pioneer in multinational programs for its clients, mostly in the field of fast-moving consumer goods. Now Professor Traverse-Healy, and teaching at universities in England, Scotland and Ireland, he formed his own consulting company after leaving Infoplan.

The earliest international pioneer among the independent agencies was John Hill of Hill & Knowlton. Hill came from Cleveland, a comparatively small city but one which has been the birthplace of other remarkable world class professional service

* This chapter is loosely based on a chapter on Public Relations Consultancy: Background and Definition contributed by the author to the book, *The Practice of Public Relations*, edited by Wilfred Howard and published by Butterworth-Heinemann.

firms – Ernst & Young, the accountants and management consultants, and the Jones Day law firm.

Hill was a reporter on the *Cleveland Plain Dealer* before crossing the line into PR and establishing the partnership with Knowlton. Hill's client, the Iron and Steel Institute, persuaded him to relocate to New York during the big steel industry strike in 1934. The story is told that at the time Hill was neither eager to move nor to undertake the assignment. So when the institute pressed him hard, he named an outrageously high fee which he was certain they would refuse.

They accepted. Hill relocated. The new New York-based firm which was to become the industry leader for many years was born. And John Hill established a pricing policy which ensured he and his associates were paid top dollar. But Knowlton remained in Cleveland and played no significant further role in the growth and success of the firm.

Hill & Knowlton entered Europe in the early 1960s but made a major impact internationally when they acquired Eric White and Associates in 1970, thus gaining a ready-made and strongly established network in the Asia Pacific region. Eric White, the founder, was an Australian who in a few years established one of the world's most potent networks, including a strong operation in London.

Hill & Knowlton was quickly followed as a firm with international ambitions by Burson-Marsteller and Daniel J. Edelman, Inc., each of which established operations in London in the 1960s.

Both Harold Burson (the PR half of the partnership; Marsteller was an advertising man) and Dan Edelman were New Yorkers, but Dan Edelman had established his firm in Chicago. Both had studied journalism and served during World War II in the US Army's psychological warfare section, perhaps the perfect grounding for the profession both were to enter after the war.

Burson's early strength was its work for industrial companies which were attracted by the combination of media relations, trade press advertising and printed brochures the firm supplied. Edelman, on the other hand, was the acknowledged leader in public relations for consumer products and gained fame in the USA as the creator of the media tour – a PR technique in which a company spokesperson visited key markets, performed store openings, did radio and newspaper interviews and, most important of all, participated in a talk show on local television.

Now both companies offer their clients a complete range of specialist PR services from offices in most key centers around the world.

Another giant of international PR had his career shaped during the war, France's Jacques Coup de Frejac. While he always gives recognition to the leadership of the USA in most PR techniques, he opened the minds of many people in France, Europe and beyond to the importance of communications. Perhaps more important, he played a major role in encouraging clients in the US and UK to understand the French market and the European movement. De Frejac was the name given to Jacques Coup when he joined the French Resistance. He was only 18 years old when he served as aide de camp to General de Gaulle in the early years of World War II.

In the 1980s Hill & Knowlton, Burson Marsteller and Edelman were joined by a new – and differently constructed competitor – Shandwick. The newcomer was different in two obvious ways. First, it was founded in Britain, by Peter Gummer. Second, it was a publicly held company, its shares listed on the London stock exchange. The big three American multinationals were privately held (until Burson Marsteller was bought by Young & Rubicam and Hill & Knowlton by J. Walter Tompson).

Peter Gummer (now Lord Chadlington) used a strong UK base of operations built from a number of autonomous units practicing financial and investor relations, public affairs and consumer PR and the availability of finance from Shandwick's status as a public company to launch a major buying spree of 35 agencies in the USA, Europe and the Far East.

A combination of Shandwick "paper" and cash enabled Gummer to achieve an international presence in a fraction of the time it had taken others to assemble their networks.

Shandwick owed its strength in the Asia-Pacific to the vision and industry of another of the titans of international public relations – Taiji Kohara. The Japanese PR doyen was to his region what John Hill, Dan Edelman and Harold Burson were to the USA, Tim Traverse-Healy and Jacques Coup de Frejac to Europe and Eric White to Australia.

Having started his own company in Tokyo in 1968 Kohara went on to establish International Public Relations (IPR), an immensely strong network of offices in 43 countries stretching from Japan to Australia, which Shandwick acquired in 1988 for a price estimated to be $45 million.

The majority of PR budgets in the early years were within the control of the marketing departments of business organizations. Given that they were generally allotted as a tiny percentage of the advertising budgets, it was natural that these public relations or publicity programs were entrusted to the advertising agency. It was, after all, staffed with skilled communicators who were seen as being able to do the job required. Moreover, because they controlled the larger advertising budget, it was often assumed, if not said aloud, that they exercised considerable leverage over the media, and this would ensure the desired level of editorial publicity.

The advertising agencies took on staff as the demand for public relations services increased and established special departments. In due course, these grew into separate subsidiary companies engaged exclusively in public relations. The proper fees and costs could now be established for the services which had grown too great to be given free to large advertisers. Because they were in close contact with client organizations, and they had resources of finance and ancillary services of design, production and printing, the public relations divisions, or subsidiary companies of the large advertising agencies, established themselves as the largest "agencies" in the US and Western Europe.

While these developments were taking place, a number of independent public relations agencies were launched and were gaining in reputation. Some specialized in a specific branch, others were generalist. they had a great strength-building challenge, outside their skills as publicists: they had to survive on what they could earn by providing public relations advice and services. They had to become viable businesses, charging realistic fees covering all their costs and leaving profits for investment. Unless they managed this, they would cease to exist.

Many not only managed to exist – they flourished, and took over the leadership from the advertising agency offshoots. But the advertising agencies were not to be outdone, and ultimately once again achieved a dominant ownership position in the field of public relations. In the early 1980s, three large, international PR agencies were acquired by advertising agencies anxious to re-establish themselves in public relations. Further acquisitions of major PR firms have taken place in the second half of the 1990s. Now, eight of the world's largest PR companies are owned by advertising agencies; another, Shandwick PLC, is a publicly traded company on the London Stock Exchange; and Edelman Public Relations Worldwide is independent and privately owned by the Edelman family and senior executives of the company.

The description "public relations agency" today is suitable, but still less than accurate, for the majority of firms. While there are a number of people practicing as consultants only (they do not engage in the practical implementation of the advice and strategies they recommend), the majority of public relations companies are both consultants and agents. This is the reason why, together with the origins of ad agency public relations divisions, the public relations agency is usually referred to as "the agency".

For the majority of agencies, there are two clearly defined roles:

1. The provision of expert and objective advice to clients based on a knowledge of the mechanisms that will affect the opinion of key publics, allied to a good knowledge of those clients' organizations, their industries and markets. In this, the consultant will draw on his and his firm's experience gained from previous assignments of a similar nature.
2. To act as the public relations agent of the client, assuming responsibility for executing agreed-upon programs on the client's behalf. This might involve, for example, the establishment of an information office for the client, the provision of public relations personnel, the production of various printed and videotaped materials, the execution of events, and the conduct of media relations and publicity efforts.

Often one agency will fulfill both roles, with the senior staff (partners or directors) providing the consulting or counseling service and then involving other executive staff in the agency function. It is not unusual, however, for a client organization to retain the services of more than one agency to meet its needs for advice on the one hand – often specialist in nature – and executional services on the other.

■ Types of agency

A large proportion of modern agencies could describe themselves as "full service," in that they have staffs with a blend of experience that enable them to offer both consulting and agency services across the different "specialties" within public relations – for example, media relations, technical communications, government relations, employee communications, international communications and marketing support. Even if the full range of highly qualified specialist advice is not available within the agency, the "full service" firm will, in most instances, be able to bring the necessary qualified person into its team as a part-time advisor.

The 1970s saw the rapid development of a number of strictly specialist agencies. The description "specialist" can be applied in a number of ways.

There are agencies which specialize in particular branches of industry; examples are firms which operate exclusively in the field of health and medicine, or those which confine themselves to clients involved in travel, tourism and related activities, and yet more which concentrate on fashion, beauty, household products and food.

More generally, however, specialization means that the firm restricts itself to one of the sub-specializations of public relations such a financial communications, government relations and employee and community relations. Chapter 7 deals more fully with specialized fields of public relations.

■ Public relations agency structures

Although some of the largest PR agencies are now owned by ad agencies, most continue to operate as autonomous units. And the majority of public relations agencies are privately owned limited companies. It is perhaps surprising that, with aspirations to professional status, this form of corporate structure for public relations firms should be the norm, rather than the partnership structure to be found in the accounting and legal professions. In the case of the few public companies, senior members of the staff are often board directors and it is not unusual for them to be shareholders as well. Whether public, ad agency-owned, or private, most public relations companies have some method of profit-sharing to enable at least the senior staff to participate in the success of the enterprise.

Because the origins of many public relations companies are linked with advertising agencies, it is common, but an error, to compare structures and costs between these two branches of communications. Public relations agencies are closer, in many ways, to management consultants, accounting and law firms. They charge fees related to the time spent on client work. Although most agencies charge an additional commission on production costs, this mainly reflects the administrative costs of overseeing production and is not the principal source of income.

There are two main kinds of operational structure within public relations agencies as related to client service. The following examples relate to typical full-service rather than specialist agencies.

The first, and less usual nowadays, is the functional structure. This has an obvious relation to the usual advertising agency structure. Primary consultants and program supervisors are usually called account directors or supervisors. Their job is to advise clients, develop the strategy, budget and method of operation for the programs, and then mobilize the resources of the agency and its subcontractors.

In a functionally structured agency, the staff are specialists in one or another aspect of public relations and invariably work on all the agency's clients, under the supervision of the account director. Take for example a program with extensive demands for a wide range of actions, including an intensive press relations campaign, a strong effort with local radio stations, a briefing for elected officials and an audio-visual presentation for general use. The account director will brief the head of the agency's press office, the specialist whose sole task is working with radio and TV, the public affairs specialist and an executive from the audio-visual and film section. In my view, while the merits of the functional system are clear, the disadvantages only become obvious in practice. Too many people are involved, those responsible for the actual execution do not have close enough contact with the client and, in general, the time of the account director and the functional executives is spread across too wide a range of projects for sufficient commitment and attention to be given to each. Another problem is that the person aspiring to a broad career in public relations can easily get trapped in a single functional department.

The more usual structure now is that of the account group, in which the account director and one or more executives are responsible for a group of clients whose interests are in some way related.

Many agencies form their account groups by public relations specialty (rather than functional specialty). They will have, for example, account groups for clients whose needs are in investor relations, and others for government relations, technical and industrial public relations, consumer marketing public relations, and so on. The heads of these groups might have started as specialists but they will have been trained and have developed over time as competent all-around consultants and executives. Alternatively, they may have started as all-rounders but then developed a specialist skill. In such an agency, the top management will have discussed the client's needs fully with him. If the work is largely, say, public affairs, the client will be served by the government relations group. The head of this group will offer consulting services and will also undertake or supervise directly much of the day-to-day work of the program. If the client is large and the program involves intensive activity in, say, government relations, investor relations and marketing public relations, the work will be divided into three programs undertaken by three different groups, with a management coordinator appointed to oversee the total quality of service to the client. Such account groups are, in effect, mini-agencies, and in many cases are managed as profit centers. They provide an opportunity to learn teamwork and offer training for senior management positions.

■ Public relations consultancy costs

Agencies are in business to make a profit for shareholders and a good living for their staff, as well as to offer service to clients. In general, they seek to make an overall profit from income of between 10 and 20 per cent before tax from the fees they charge clients. Dividends to shareholders and profit-sharing to staff are paid from this profit. The balance goes to finance the growth of the agency and provide it with the necessary reserves to ensure stability. Thus an agency with an income of $10,000,000 per annum might expect to make a pre-tax profit of $1,500,000. A part of that – say, $500,000 – might be allocated for profit-sharing or an annual bonus. A prudent board might also have invested say $250,000 in new equipment as the likely profit became known. Of the remaining balance of $750,000, close to 40 per cent ($300,000) will go toward taxes, leaving $450,000 to cover dividends and cash to be retained in the business. This will be needed to finance cash flow and growth.

To achieve that profit, however, requires good management and adherence to a pricing policy.

Staff salaries are the largest single cost of an agency. Surveys of members of the Public Relations Consultants Association (PRCA) have shown that in nearly all agencies staff salaries are around 50 per cent of income. So our "sample" $10,000,000 agency will have an annual salary bill of $5,000,000.

The second largest single cost (usually about 10 per cent) is rent. Then come all the other costs, such as telephone, travel, entertaining, hiring and training, which should not amount to more than another 35 per cent if 15 per cent profit is to be made.

When an agency discusses its costs openly with clients, it seldom has difficulties in getting fees appropriate to the assignment.

Following are the main fee systems in operation.

Fixed fee. This is negotiated annually with the client, based on historical knowledge of the volume of work and time involved, or is estimated based on agency experience with similar programs. The fee is usually paid monthly.

Retainer fee and hourly or *per diem* **charges.** In this system, clients pay a very modest retainer fee, which means they can draw on the agency's services when needed, but the retainer does not automatically "buy" any service and it is payable even if no work is done. When service is needed, an agreed-upon hourly rate is charged to the client. This might be broken down by the hours put in by specific individuals, for example one rate for a senior consultant, another for a junior staff member, and shown as such to the client on the invoice. It is also quite usual for a uniform "team" time rate to be established, which reflects the average of the combined time of senior consultants, executives and support staff. In certain countries, hourly rates are established and recommended by national public relations institutes.

Minimum fee and hourly charges. This approach is often confused with the retainer system because of similarities, but there are significant differences. The minimum fee is invariably more substantial than the retainer. It reflects the fact that the agency has calculated that it is likely to spend a given amount of time each month working for the client and has assigned the staff to do so. The hourly charge comes into operation when the basic time has been used up. Thus, when clients pay a minimum fee of $10,000 per month for, say, 50 hours work at $200 per hour, and the actual time expended in the month is 60 hours, the bill for that month will be $12,000. In a month when only 40 hours work is done, the minimum fee of $10,000 is still payable. Sometimes there is a quarterly "equalization" system built in, to reflect the ups and downs that are inevitable.

It is normal for agencies to charge subcontract, production and out-of-pocket costs, in addition to the professional fee.

■ Working with the client

In most respects, the working day and practical duties of public relations agency executives are similar to those of their equivalents in the public relations departments of their clients. The likelihood is that the agency people will find themselves working in close cooperation with a public relations professional or at least an experienced communicator within the client organization.

Until the mid-1960s, it was normal for clients embarking on public relations programs to make a decision either to retain an external agency or to employ a public relations executive internally. Now it is relatively common for the larger, forward-looking organizations to have established internal public relations departments and for these to retain the services of an agency in addition.

In the case of well-staffed client PR departments, the prime need is for expert, objective external PR consultants. In other cases where the internal staff is small but there is going to be extra work over a defined period, it makes sense to retain specific agency services.

■ Qualities of good PR consultants

Over and above the qualities needed by *all* public relations practitioners, following are those required of agency executives:

- Observe the successes and failures of techniques employed for other clients and bring this knowledge and experience to bear for the benefit of clients they are currently serving.
- Achieve mastery and knowledge of the subcontracting services available to the agency that will benefit clients.
- Use the resources and expertise of other professionals within the agency when faced with a complex problem.
- Sharpen their creative edge by maintaining regular contact with other professionals in the firm.
- Maintain strong powers of analysis, presentation and creativity, because an agency has to sell its services in competition with other agencies. In short, consultants have to win the right to practice public relations.
- Understand budgeting and business management, vital elements for a career in a PR organization.
- Keep abreast of media developments, new communications techniques and the current mood of public opinion on a variety of issues, if their advice is to be valued as smart, objective and reliable.
- Manage their own time expertly, allocating it appropriately among client contact, program execution, monitoring results, reporting to the client and maintaining direct contact with the media and other publics. Though difficult, the right time blend must be achieved because the client pays for a combination of expertise and time.

CHAPTER 14

Research

Business executives underpin planning with research. No new product is launched without extensive market research. New plant siting requires researching community attitudes.

Entering new markets is never done without pre-testing potential benefits and downsides. The effective PR executive must be in step with the business research phenomenon.

An aspiring international public relations executive needs to master research in all its forms.

He must know the different research specialties and when to use them. He must know how to develop questionnaires; structure simple research projects; and the strengths and weaknesses of the specialist research organizations for the occasions when a project must be subcontracted. He must learn where research already exists and can be bought at a reasonable price so that he can avoid wasting money.

Furthermore, he must understand the value of quantitative vs. qualitative research, statistically projective vs. anecdotal research, focus groups vs. phone surveys, literature searches and market research, demographics and psychographics.

Above all, he must be able to interpret the findings produced by all kinds of research projects so that the data can be effectively used at the outset in the development of public relations programs.

That research has become critical to public relations is reflected in the criteria set by major PR awards competitions around the world. Virtually all require a research section which sets out the scope of the challenge or opportunity facing the organization. The last section of an entry, devoted to the results and evaluation of the program that has been entered, is expected to link back to the initial research findings, demonstrating what has been achieved. No program, however creative the central idea or brilliant the execution, is likely to walk off with the prize if the research section is weak.

The attention that is now paid to research is an important sign of the "growing up" of public relations. PR is all too often criticized (I am sorry to say, with good reason) by others in other business specialties for being too "instinctive" or "seat of the pants". PR practitioners in the past have been unable to hold a strong position in debates on policy, direction or creative content of communications programs because their ideas and interventions were not grounded in the research and analysis that appeared to be the hallmark of others, especially those from management consultancies, marketing and advertising agencies.

PR people were also less prepared to be accountable by any concrete form of measurement and evaluation. This had the effect of devaluing the perception of the contribution PR could make as a component in any integrated communications project.

Another factor has militated against widespread use of research for PR programming – cost. The cost of undertaking a reliable, thorough research study to establish the effect of a PR program can be prohibitive. In some instances, research cost is greater than the cost of the PR effort itself. As a consequence, until recently research was seldom undertaken. That has gradually changed as the size of PR programs has grown, along with the costs of PR advice and program implementation. Because good upfront research sets up the need for a PR program, the executives proposing the PR budget will not get approvals unless they provide adequate research underpinning and measurement of results, and the research cost is at an acceptable ratio to the basic PR costs.

Historically, an inability to prove the tremendous cost:benefit ratio of public relations in relation to other communications techniques left the PR manager with a tiny slice of the marketing communications pie and, sometimes, no slice at all – especially compared to the large allotments for advertising.

If a basic knowledge of research is important for every PR practitioner, there are additional compelling reasons for competency on the part of those engaged in international communications.

While research can add to specific knowledge in single-country work, it might be possible – in a small and homogenous country – for a practitioner to have enough accumulated knowledge of the population, trends, geographical differences and other data to construct a program that will be generally on target.

But, on a worldwide basis, where you will be expected to make decisions about programs being undertaken in countries of which you have no first-hand knowledge and which you may not even have visited, a research-based foundation for your programs is essential.

Research then is vital both as a tool that will enable you to assess the situation you face as you start your PR activities as well as a form of measurement at periodic intervals to check whether your progress is satisfactory. Where can help be found?

There is a variety of resources available to the PR practitioners covering many specialist fields of research. There is almost certain to be research already available or new studies that may be commissioned that will be relevant to you in the huge range of activities covered under the heading of PR.

This chapter does not attempt to be a primer on research for the PR executive. There are other books and courses available for anyone wanting to study the subject at length. I hope to provide a helpful guide for the person who needs to know where to go for data and would like to know of money-saving short cuts, if they exist.

(Note: Research is also covered briefly in chapter 3, on Corporate Reputation Management, and in chapter 8, Issue Identification and Management.)

■ Check existing sources

Quite likely, some of the data you need already exists. It is just a matter of finding out where, and if it is available to you.

It will be very much like looking for a suit.

Clearly, your best choice would be to go along to the finest tailor, get measured up, choose your cloth and have the garment cut and stitched to fit you perfectly. This carries a high price, appropriate for the degree of skill, personal attention and customization it is given.

But excellent, serviceable and high-quality suits can be found ready-to-wear. In many cases you can mix and match trousers and jackets, or find "not quite finished suits" which can be altered to be almost like a bespoke article. Research products exist that are identical to the custom-tailored, near-ready and ready-to-wear suits.

Ultimately, you can also find a second-hand suit which might be ideal. You might not like such a suit in your wardrobe; you would not worry quite so much were you to find some piece of research which tells you what you need to know but has been paid for by someone else.

The first place to look is at home.

Large companies are the repositories of huge amounts of data. Most of it has been acquired over the years by various departments and seldom is it concentrated in one place. It is not uncommon for different divisions to be questioning the same people – even for different departments in a division to do so – without being aware that the other is doing so. Data is accumulated by one brand that is not necessarily shared with other brands. Your first step must be to question the person responsible in the central research department archive (if such exists). Step two: is to contact company PR and marketing people to establish what recent studies they have undertaken. They will likely have an Aladdin's cave of information about the market trends, your company's or brand's position in the market, its qualities and comparisons with competitors.

What you find may enable you to proceed without commissioning additional research because you will be able to piggy-back on these studies. And even if you decide you need additional data, the available information will help you focus your new studies more accurately and thus save time and money.

Make sure you contact the chief financial officer. You will find he also has a storehouse of information, starting with reports of analysts from financial institutions. It is their job to know more about your company than you know yourself and to rate it against its competitors, and they have the resources to find out. In their periodic reports, you get superb appraisals of your industry and insights into your own company. And it all comes FREE.

The CFO might also consult you, if you are responsible for investor relations, for other data that might of great importance to him. Most public companies want to know the names of the people who own their shares. While this data is of limited use in tranquil times, if a merger or hostile bid is likely, it becomes exceptionally important that the company be able to reach out to shareholders whose holdings are in the names of nominees. Then it is useful to know who is behind the nominees so that you can reach them with the specifically targeted information that you know will help them to make the right decision – as you see it. There are a number of companies that do this work on the international stock exchanges, among them: Corporate Investor Communications, Inc., Carson Group, Technimetrics, D.F. King & Co. and First Chicago Trust Company.

■ Historical data from continuous studies

Check out the major research companies for the historical data that is available from the studies that they may have been conducting continuously over several years.

You may be surprised to find that your company or brand has been included for comparison purposes in the regular panel audits that AC Nielsen conducts in shops and the home, or in a variety of research projects routinely undertaken by Gallup, ORC, MORI, Harris Polls and others. This will give you a head start in establishing your current position. All you need to do is to join the study – and pay up – to establish how your PR work is changing the company or brand perception.

One such study of special importance to public relations practitioners is undertaken periodically by Yankelovich in the USA. It surveys a large number of journalists and editors from all forms of general and specialist media on a number of topics. Useful enough in itself to PR executives, the study allows subscribers to ask specific questions and include their own trade media. The survey can help you ascertain how strong the relationship is between company and its key media, and find out what techniques are working well and which are not. It also rates the company's media relations performance against its main competitors.

■ Societies, ruling bodies and other organizations

You may be called upon to become an instant expert in some special population sector. For example, someone might propose that a PR program be undertaken that involves anglers or hobby fishermen, or perhaps mountain bikers.

The best sources – and the least costly – are always the ruling bodies or societies that serve these interest groups. The society or association will usually send you at no charge beyond postage a wealth of material containing demographic and psychographic information about its members. This will quickly help you establish just how useful a group it will be to your company. More often than not, nowadays, the information from these societies is also available from the websites they maintain.

In the major PR field of healthcare communications, a prime source of data can be the patient support groups that exist in most countries and are very well organized. Examples are patient associations for people suffering from kidney ailments, heart conditions, cancer, MS, diabetes, AIDS and other illnesses. In addition to being a source of information, these groups can be excellent partners in communications initiatives, offering a direct and highly targeted channel to a group of people of specific interest to you.

A secondary source is the journals serving these interest groups.

■ Country information

Those practicing PR on an international scale will often want to gain objective information about a specific country to match with the information being presented by the company representatives there.

The first port of call should be to the local embassy or consulate general of that country, which will usually provide you with a great deal of useful information about the country. From this you can build up your own picture, perhaps in advance of a visit. The second should be the Foreign Office or Department of Trade (Export) of your own country's government. You will find that they usually have a wealth of knowledge about overseas markets and will also give you their opinion on such important matters as the political stability of the country and even some do's and don'ts of doing business there. Remember, you have paid for this through your taxes, so you have a right to the help from your own public servants. Mostly, they are glad to oblige.

You should complement this by requesting the most recent study undertaken of that country by the Economist Intelligence Unit, which will be available at a cost of around $200. Or collect the most recent advertising-supported "special report" or supplement on that country published by *The Economist*, the *Wall Street Journal*, the *Financial Times* or another reputable and serious journal.

Some of the very best country-by-country business profiles are published by the world-renowned consulting firm Ernst & Young in a series of books intended to be very informative to prospective investors or those doing business there.

■ Caravans

Caravans are regular researches undertaken weekly or monthly by many specialist research organizations under contract to major corporations. These track product purchases, opinions and voting intentions. The skill of the research organization goes into selecting small panels on a so-called random basis (that is anything but random), which will reflect the demographics of the population as a whole. As a PR executive you should master the interpretation of results gleaned from these caravan studies.

In addition, you should also exploit the opportunity presented by the fact that the research company undertaking the study almost certainly has covered its cost and is making a profit before you even sign up. For a relatively small cost, you should be able to negotiate up to five additional questions relevant to you. This achieves a limited custom-tailored research which might well have been out of reach if you were the sole sponsor of the study.

PR people who are knowledgeable and alert know that research data is one of the magical routes to winning coverage in the media, which has an insatiable appetite for information about what people think or do. So in addition to using caravan research as an economical way of finding out data of real importance to the construction of a PR program and its key messages, use additional questions on caravans to generate data that will be appetizing to the media and can be linked to the product, corporation or theme for which you want to achieve publicity.

■ Focus groups

Focus-group testing is probably the research format of most importance to public relations practitioners. The information one can gain is highly qualitative and detailed.

Beyond learning how people feel about a certain product, person or concept, the skilled researcher can establish the strength of feeling, and the ease with which that opinion might be altered and how that might be done. Focus groups, because they involve people for several hours – for which they get paid a fee – are also able to establish the acceptability of alternative product offerings and ideas.

This method is routinely used by politicians and political parties to check how the public might react to various initiatives.

Most important for people in the public relations field, focus groups are the testing ground for ideas and messages, the grist for the mill of all who practice communications.

All focus groups can be useful when interpreted with skill and intelligence. But the methods sheltering under this uniform description can range widely. You might have a fairly simple gathering of a group of people who are a representative sample, in a conference room at your company or agency or research firm, or even in an hotel room rented for the purpose. At the other end of the range, you have the use of custom-built research centers fitted with microphoned rooms behind one-way mirrors and "voting" buttons through which the panelists can give instant responses to questions put by a focus-group facilitator. There is great value for the PR practitioner to attend the more sophisticatedly-organized focus groups. Attendance offers a marked heightening of understanding of human reactions to the issues raised, as compared with a later reading of the written results.

A well-run focus-group study is a superb navigational tool for the PR practitioner aspiring to chart the course for a successful communications program. It can establish your exact position on the map at the starting point. It will tell you the course you must set to reach your destination. It will suggest course corrections. It will also tell you the blind alleys and the way that is fraught with dangers and obstacles. And, if used periodically, it will tell you your progress and chart your new position. Finally, it will tell you when you have reached your destination.

When British Airways (BA) decided it wanted to acquire a substantial shareholding in US Air to establish a strategic alliance that would benefit both airlines, a coalition headquartered in the USA was immediately established to fight the plan. The influence of American Airlines, United Airlines, Delta and Federal Express was formidable and their publicity machine was quickly mobilized to tell the story of the damage that would be caused, along with the threat to security, employment and the American economy.

BA realized that they had a fight on their hands. They were going to get no points or thanks for stepping in and offering a new lease on life to an airline that appeared to have no future. American law prevented the acquisition of any US carrier by a foreign entity and there was a gray area around even minority holdings if they could be shown to transfer effective control of the airline into foreign hands. So the opposition coalition challenged even BA's intention to take a minority interest, suggesting it was the thin end of the wedge, and in any case, the investment promised by BA would give it *de facto* control, exercised from behind the curtain.

BA knew they would have to assemble an influential group of allies if the US government watchdog organizations were not to be steamrolled by the opposition group.

They listed all the benefits that would emerge from the strategic alliance if it were to be approved. These included benefits to flyers such as a single ticket, baggage transfers and neat connections to destinations worldwide from all points served by US Air in the USA; increased tourism opportunity for customers flying in from Europe; a certain future for US Air instead of the possibility of its failure financially; a prospect of continuing prosperity and good airline service for the many towns and cities in the Northeast of the USA; and, finally, the safety of the many jobs that were at risk.

At the outset it was hard to know which of these arguments, and others, would prove the most compelling.

But soon there was no contest. Focus-group testing in several of US Air's regional centers came to one conclusion. There was only one issue at stake. Jobs.

And jobs, jobs, jobs.

The message was clear. Passenger benefits, increased inward tourism and all other good results of the strategic alliance would play second fiddle to the constant theme of jobs. The BA–US Air alliance would assure the jobs of people in the many communities served by US Air. Not only would this resonate in those places and with their local political leaders, it was also the key issue for decision makers in Washington, DC.

Jobs became the theme of the campaign, which succeeded in its goals, with BA taking a significant minority shareholding in US Air.

In the years that have gone by since that achievement, US Air has returned to respectable profits and even changed its name. But BA has raised it sights and has established a new strategic alliance with the much larger American Airlines, so as to be a stronger force in the new competitive arena where it is imperative to be a global airline power to assure a successful future.

■ Copy and ad testing

Focus groups are used regularly by advertisers to test alternative copy and creative concepts but very few PR creative ideas are subjected to similar, rigorous, routine trials. If and when PR creative testing becomes more common, many unsuccessful campaigns will be eliminated before they cause embarrassment and a waste of time and money.

■ Clip count and analysis

While the ultimate result of the work of the PR practitioner can only be established through awareness and opinion research conducted with the target groups he is seeking to influence, resources are not always available to undertake studies of the necessary scale and frequency. Moreover, changing of awareness and opinions is most often the result of several factors – perhaps a combination of advertising, direct mail, word of mouth and editorial coverage. All organizations should try to establish the relative impact of each of these techniques so that the investment and weight of effort can be adjusted as necessary.

For this purpose PR executives must measure the output of their work.

Some assumptions can be made: if the number of communications that take place – whether in the form of speaking engagements, newsletters or videos distributed, interviews conducted, articles published, and TV and radio broadcasts aired – is at a high level, then the awareness of your company or product will be correspondingly high.

And, if the content of these communications is broadly positive, then listeners, readers and viewers will most likely react positively to that information.

There is a variety of services in the world's larger markets that offer media analysis in varying degrees of sophistication. Most of the clippings services, which in years past merely clipped and sent in packets of cuttings on a weekly basis, now offer enhanced analysis. On request and the payment of an additional fee, they will provide a classification of the content of each press report. The most basic of these services will tell you if the report is negative, neutral or positive, and the information is presented in easy-to-look-at graphic format, useful for presentation purposes to wider audiences.

Analysis will also document how, over a period of time, it is possible to establish an improving trend (from negative toward positive coverage) or the opposite. This allows the PR director to take appropriate action.

One specialist media analysis firm which has been increasing its international representation is CARMA.

The following case study for CARMA International client, Disneyland Paris, outlines an example of how media analysis was used to help justify PR to senior management, help refine strategy and demonstrate value to the bottom line. It shows how the volume and favorability of media coverage could increase the number of visitors to the facility.

Coverage for Disneyland Paris was cyclical – which is how they wanted it – to stimulate visitors in the warm summer months, and not to compete with the US during Europe's gray winters. Disney's strategy was to maintain a steady momentum

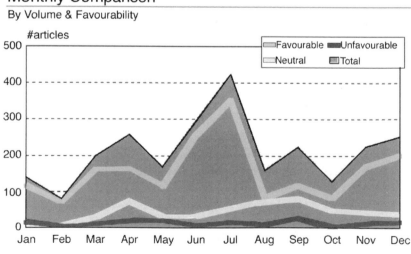

Monthly Comparison
By Volume & Favourability

Chart 14.1

of good-news stories – which they had with the successful launch of Spacemountain – and to restrict negative comment.

Proactive Communications - Monthly Comparison

By Volume

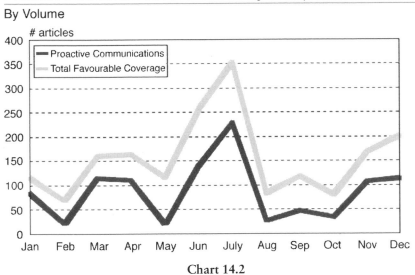

Chart 14.2

You get out of PR what you put into it – no one will do you any favors unless you work at it. This chart proves the point. It also shows that without PR, there would only be mis-information, bland and/or negative articles.

Leading Attraction Issues

By Volume, Favourability & Favourability Rating

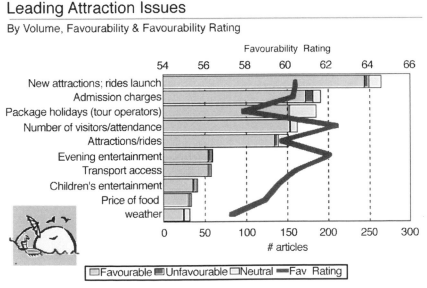

Chart 14.3

But it's not just about volume or favorability. It is also about CONTENT. What are the "hot buttons" for the press, what is moving up and down the agenda and where are the strong and weak spots?

Leading Positive Messages Comparison

By Volume

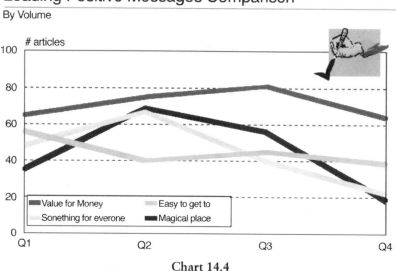

Chart 14.4

Leading Negative Messages Comparison

By Volume

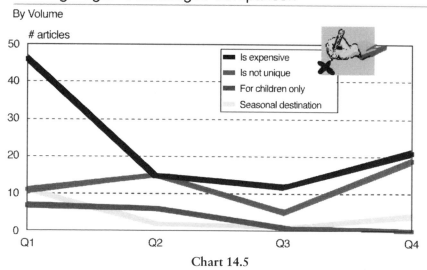

Chart 14.5

And it's also about MESSAGES – showing the client how successful or not they are in distinguishing themselves from the competition – and what are the growing trends they need to address.

Demographic Analysis

Opportunities to See During 1995 & Favourability

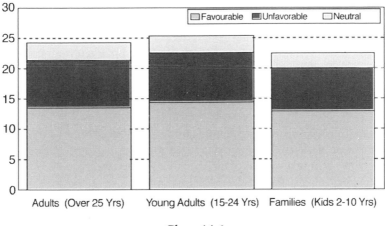

Chart 14.6

Disney also used the media information to help with planning and targeting. They must do more to concentrate on getting good coverage in the media that reach families with young children.

UK Attendance Figures

Comparison Against No. of Articles

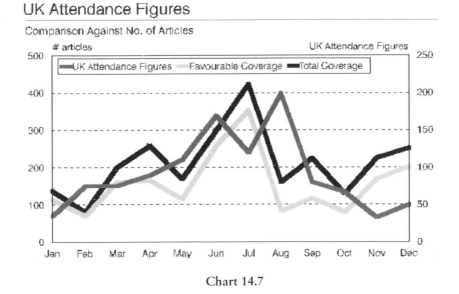

Chart 14.7

More important, they need to know that their PR is working – by showing that good PR does make a difference where it matters, to the bottom line, by driving visitor attendance from one of the many key markets.

"The definition of evaluation through media analysis like CARMA's should be a wide definition. Evaluating public relations campaigns is just the ABC of the whole alphabet, the first notes of the symphony," concludes Sandra MacLeod, managing director/Europe for CARMA. "But the profile of the whole company from the perspective of every stakeholder, internal and external, should be our target."

"Only that way will we really have our radar trained on every aspect of our business, ready to catch every opportunity, and every threat, from wherever it comes."

■ Continuous interactive image tracking

Some international companies are now installing interactive brand awareness tracking studies in major markets. These provide real-time information.

They involve setting up panels of individuals equipped with the electronic response terminals. They record their awareness and opinions of a company or brands at regular intervals. By matching the increase or decrease in awareness, it is possible to identify the impact of various promotional events, conferences, advertising, special offers or PR initiatives.

These methods of monitoring public reactions are important enough on a day-by-day basis. But they increase in value in times of crisis or when there is a major burst of negative media coverage. The day-by-day responses can provide the skilled PR operative with a vital navigational aid. The data can be used to determine whether to adopt a low-key containment policy or whether to become proactive. What's more, those strategies can be varied from region to region, as this kind of research can pinpoint where an event has caused a major furor and where it has passed unnoticed.

Index